Positive Discipline
in the Classroom

## Other books in the Developing Capable People series:

▼

# Positive Discipline in the Classroom

How to Effectively Use Class Meetings
and Other Positive Discipline Strategies

Jane Nelsen, Ed.D.
Lynn Lott, M.A., M.F.C.C.
H. Stephen Glenn

 **Prima Publishing**
P.O. Box 1260BK
Rocklin, CA 95677
(916) 786-0426

Production by Jennifer Boynton, Bookman Productions
Copyediting by Elizabeth Dilernia
Interior design by Renee Deprey and Suzanne Montazer
Typography by Bookends Typesetting
Cover design by The Dunlavey Studio

Lyrics from the song "Number One" are reprinted with permission from *Songs for Elementary Emotional Development* by Wayne Frieden and Marie Hartwell-Walker. Copyright 1992 by Education Research Associates, P.O. Box 7678-J, Amherst, MA 01004.

**Library of Congress Cataloging-in-Publication Data**

Nelsen, Jane.
    Positive discipline in the classroom / Jane Nelsen, Lynn Lott, and H. Stephen Glenn.
      p.  cm.
    Includes index.
    ISBN 1-55958-311-8 : $14.95
    1. Classroom management—United States.  2. School discipline—United States.  I. Lott, Lynn.  II. Glenn, H. Stephen.
III. Title.
LB3013.N4 1993                    92–42951
371.5′3—dc20                 CIP

93  94  95  96  97  RRD  10 9 8 7 6 5 4 3 2 1

Printed in the United States of America

**How to Order:**

Quantity discounts are available from Prima Publishing, P.O. Box 1260BK, Rocklin, CA 95677; telephone (916) 786-0426. On your letterhead include information concerning the intended use of the books and the number of books you wish to purchase.

*To Alfred Adler and Rudolf Dreikurs, for their theories
of mutual respect, and to the hundreds of school
personnel and students who have confirmed the value of
these theories in schools.*

*A special thanks to those people who have taken our
ideas and used them in more creative ways than we ever
imagined.*

▼

# Contents

# Contents

▼

# Introduction

**T**housands of young people lose their first job after school, not because they lack knowledge, but because they lack skills to deal with other people. They have not learned to work efficiently within a system in which they have to take responsibility for the consequences of their choices and actions. Each year, American businesses spend millions of dollars on remedial education for entry-level employees, mainly to teach them to understand their responsibilities within the system, as well as how to think, speak, and interact with others.

We often hear the cry, "Back to basics!" We agree. However, we disagree with many on their definition of "the basics." We do not believe the basics are reading, writing, and arithmetic. We believe the basics are courage, confidence, and life skills. When children have *these* basics, they have fertile ground upon which to learn academics, and to live successfully in the world.

In the United States, the federal law requiring children to attend school says nothing about reading, writing, and arithmetic; it says that the purpose of education is "to prepare children for responsible citizenship." Reading, writing, and arithmetic do not prepare young people for responsible citizenship. All the academic knowledge in the world will not help those who lack self-discipline, judgment, social interest, the ability to make good choices, and the sense of responsibility that enables them to act effectively in life. Unfortunately, our educational system today simply does not provide young people with these skills.

In *Positive Discipline in the Classroom,* we emphasize the importance of class meetings. We have discovered that class meetings teach essential skills and empower young people with a positive attitude for success in all areas of life— school, work, family, and society. Effective class meetings prepare students for responsible citizenship. Students learn social skills, such as listening, taking turns, hearing different points of view, negotiating, communicating, helping one another, and taking responsibility for their own behavior. They also strengthen their academic skills, perhaps without realizing it. During class meetings, students learn oral language skills, attentiveness, critical-thinking skills, decision-making skills, problem-solving skills, and democratic procedures—all of which will enhance their academic performance. Many teachers find that the class-meeting process exceeds curriculum goals for social studies, language development, and health and safety, because student involvement in problem solving leads to deeper understanding and commitment to appropriate action.

After students acquire the skills they can learn through class meetings, reading, writing, and arithmetic are more meaningful in their lives. The experience of class meetings helps students become more receptive to learning what the educational system has to offer.

For years, we've watched as schools look for methods to handle classroom discipline. When the underlying motivation of discipline is control and punishment rather than an opportunity for learning, little will be accomplished. What has happened in many of our schools is sad and frightening. In a workshop at the North American Society of Adlerian Psychologists in June 1992, Dr. William Nicoll discussed the "pathological environment" created in many of our schools. With some irony, he identified "new categories" of mental illness that are created in the school environment.

Dr. Nicoll calls his first category Classroom-Induced School Phobia. This condition expresses itself by persistent, excessive worry about school and a fear of doing something or acting in a way that could be humiliating or embarrassing, possibly resulting in disapproval or rejection. The problem may be accompanied by headaches, stomach aches, decreased social functioning outside school, verbalized fears of poor performance, fear of the teacher, nightmares, sleep disturbances, depression, and a refusal to attend school.

After describing several more school-induced anxiety and mood disorders, Dr. Nicoll sums up with a description of what he calls Adult Children of Dysfunctional Classrooms, or ACDCs. These adults become agitated when faced with new tasks, responsibilities, or challenges; they suffer flashbacks involving past classroom traumas, such as failure, perceived humiliation, and loss of prestige. ACDCs may also avoid risk taking, experience feelings of inferiority or inadequacy, or possess generalized anger and resentment toward educators.

It is possible to turn this negativity around. But it takes both time and commitment to change the atmosphere in our schools and classrooms as well as our basic beliefs about the educational system. We need to move away from a system based on competition, in which success is for the few and being a success is at someone else's expense. We must move toward developing competency and self-worth, accompanied by responsible decision making and helping one another. In this atmosphere, schools can empower young people with courage, confidence, and life skills instead of burdening them with feelings of fear and inadequacy.

We, the authors, are educators committed to providing the tools that can help teachers, administrators, and parents bring health to an unhealthy system. Together, we have over seventy-five years of experience in lecturing, writing, counseling, and teaching others to create families and classrooms where both adults and children feel encouraged and empowered to accept themselves and others and to work together for the good of all. In this book, we have combined our resources to share our ideas about how to change the school environment into an atmosphere of learning and respect.

# CHAPTER
## 1

# The Positive Discipline Dream

**W**e have a dream. The dream is about schools where young people are treated with respect and have the opportunity to learn the skills they need for a successful life. The dream is about schools where children will never experience humiliation when they fail but will instead feel empowered by the opportunity to learn from their mistakes. It is a dream about schools where students learn cooperation instead of competition, where students and teachers collaborate on solutions. The dream is about students and teachers helping one another to create an environment that inspires excitement for life and learning, because fear and feelings of inadequacy and discouragement are no longer part of the learning environment. The end result is an educational system that nurtures young people and gives them the skills and attitudes that will help them be happy, contributing members of society.

Many teachers and students have realized this dream by using methods based on mutual respect. Mutual respect requires that adults see children as people. Teachers who see students as people do not treat them as robots whose only function is to be controlled and manipulated "for their own good." They see students as valuable sources with worthwhile ideas and skills.

Mutual respect is a two-way street. It invites young people to see adults as people who need nurturing and encouragement just as much as students do. A climate for mutual respect is created when teachers allow students to become involved in ways in which they can listen to one another, take each other seriously, and work *together* to solve problems for the benefit of all.

Although there are many methods for teachers and students to work together in a climate of mutual respect, the class meeting provides the greatest potential for teaching children empowering life skills in the least amount of time. Together, students and teachers can create a classroom climate that is nurturing to both self-esteem and academic performance. For this reason, the class meeting is the basis for achieving positive discipline in the classroom and is this book's central organizing principle.

Because we understand the incredible benefits for teachers and students who use class meetings, we are amazed at the resistance from school personnel who have not yet discovered their positive effects. Following are some comments we have heard from teachers and administrators, as they briefed us before in-service trainings:

> Teachers don't want you to spend much time on class meetings. They would prefer you talk about involving kids in their education, getting kids to think for themselves and helping teachers deal with acting out students.

> Students don't like to sit around in a circle discussing problems. It's not their way.

> Don't waste our time on class meetings. Some of us teach classes that are 50 minutes long and we don't have time to waste having meetings.

2

A well-run class meeting involves students in their education, teaches them to think for themselves, and eliminates most problems with acting-out students. Those who experience belonging and significance through participation in class meetings seldom need to misbehave. (For more about misbehavior, see Chapter 6.) When they do misbehave, students can learn to help each other, usually with more effective results than when they are referred to sources outside the classroom.

Too often, if students are having difficulty in the classroom, it is assumed that there are learning disabilities or behavior problems that exist solely within the students. At other times, it is assumed that the cause lies in their families. It has become popular to "solve" these problems by sending students to the principal, counselor, or school psychologist for referral to a special education program.

When classroom teachers learn to implement effective class meetings, most problems can be successfully handled through the class-meeting process instead of being referred to other sources. Students are taught a fundamental concept: "There are enough of us here to help each other; we don't need to pass the buck." With training, students seem more willing to listen to each other than to adults. Class meetings provide a supportive atmosphere for students to become actively involved in determining their needs and implementing strategies they design to benefit everyone concerned. They can come up with wonderfully creative solutions when given the opportunity.

## The Significant Seven

Hundreds of teachers have told us that discipline problems are significantly reduced when they use class meetings. Some teachers may want to implement class meetings for this reason alone. However, we firmly believe that eliminating discipline problems is only the fringe benefit of class meetings. The major benefits are the social, academic, and life skills students experience, which can be summed up in what we call the *Significant Seven*.[1] The *Significant Seven* are three empowering perceptions and four essential skills, described below.

## Three Empowering Perceptions

1. *Perception of personal capabilities:* "I am capable."
2. *Perception of significance in primary relationships:* "I contribute in meaningful ways, and I am genuinely needed."
3. *Perception of personal power of influence over life:* "I can influence what happens to me."

## Four Essential Skills

1. *Intrapersonal skill:* the ability to understand personal emotions, to use that understanding to develop self-discipline and self-control, and to learn from experiences.
2. *Interpersonal skill:* the ability to work with others through listening, communicating, cooperating, negotiating, sharing, and empathizing.
3. *Strategic skill:* the ability to respond to the limits and consequences of everyday life with responsibility, adaptability, flexibility, and integrity.
4. *Judgment skill:* the ability to develop wisdom and evaluate situations according to appropriate values.

---

[1] A chapter on each component of the Significant Seven can be found in H. Stephen Glenn and Jane Nelsen, *Raising Self-Reliant Children in a Self-Indulgent World* (Rocklin, CA: Prima Publishing, 1989).

Students who are weak in the development of these seven significant perceptions and skills are at high risk for the serious problems of youth, such as drug abuse, teen pregnancy, suicide, delinquency, and gang involvement. Students with strength in the Significant Seven are at low risk for serious problems. Obviously, it is extremely important that young people have the opportunity to develop the Significant Seven, and the class meeting provides an excellent opportunity in the following ways:

1. To develop a *perception of personal capability,* young people need a safe climate where they can experiment with learning and behavior without judgments about success or failure, right or wrong. The class meeting can provide a safe climate where students can examine their behavior, discover how it affects others, and engage in effective problem solving.

2. To develop a *perception of significance in primary relationships,* young people need the experience of having others listen to their feelings, thoughts, and ideas and take them seriously. In class meetings, everyone has the opportunity to voice opinions and give suggestions. Students learn that they can contribute significantly to the problem-solving process and can successfully follow through on chosen suggestions.

3. To develop a *perception of power and influence over their lives,* young people need to experience an environment that emphasizes accountability and encouragement. Class meetings provide a place where kids know it's okay to make mistakes and learn from them. Students learn that it's safe to take responsibility for their mistakes, because they will not be judged. They learn to give up the victim mentality of blaming others ("The teacher gave me an *F*") and accept

an accountability mentality ("I received an *F* because I didn't do the work"). They also learn that even when they can't control what happens, they *can* control their response to what happens and their choice of resulting actions.

4. Class meetings provide an excellent opportunity for the development of *intrapersonal skills.* Young people seem more willing to listen to one another than to adults. They gain understanding of their personal emotions and behavior by hearing feedback from their classmates. In a nonthreatening climate, young people are willing to be accountable for their actions. They learn to separate their feelings from their actions and the results of their actions. They can learn that what they feel (anger, for instance) is separate from what they do (hit someone), and that while feelings are always acceptable, some actions are not. They develop self-discipline and self-control by following through with consequences or suggestions from other students.

5. Class meetings provide the best possible opportunity for young people to develop *interpersonal skills* through dialogue and sharing, listening and empathizing, cooperation, negotiation, and conflict resolution. Instead of stepping in and resolving problems for students, teachers can suggest putting the problem on the class meeting agenda, where they can work on a win/win solution together.

6. During class meetings, young people develop excellent *strategic skill* by responding to the limits and consequences of everyday life with responsibility, adaptability, flexibility, and integrity. Through the problem-solving process, they learn alternative ways to express or deal with their thoughts or feelings.

7. Young people develop *judgmental skill* only when they have opportunities and encouragement

to practice making choices and decisions in an environment that emphasizes the process of trying rather than the success or failure of the attempt. A class meeting is just such an environment. Too many adults expect children to develop wisdom and sound judgment without the opportunity to practice, make mistakes, learn, and try again. Regular class meetings give young people a lot of practice time.

When teachers understand the relevance of the Significant Seven, they know how important it is to provide students with opportunities to develop strength in these empowering perception and essential skill areas. A foundation of mutual respect and student involvement is imperative. The old methods of punishment, humiliation, and control do not work.

It is a rare teacher who does *not* see the value of teaching the skills and attitudes we have discussed in our dream to empower young people. Most teachers would prefer to give up punishment and external control if they had the skills to help students learn self-control, self-discipline, responsibility, and problem-solving skills. However, making the changes necessary to realize the dream may not be easy for teachers or for students.

## Positive Change for Future Dividends

Many teachers are accustomed to directing students, and many students are used to being directed by teachers. It takes time to break ineffective habits and replace them with empowering habits. Expect some reluctance, as you begin the process of helping students develop the capacity to solve their own problems.

One of the most difficult changes for some teachers is seeing the value of taking ten to thirty minutes out of their academic schedule to spend on class meetings. Conversely, teachers who have experienced the short- and long-range benefits wonder how they survived without these meetings. We understand the time required for class meetings and the demands placed on school personnel who have limited time in any given day to devote to what they consider "nonacademic" activities. But the benefits to both students and teachers are well worth the time and training it takes to learn effective class-meeting skills.

Some classroom teachers are reluctant to start one more new thing. Others think they will be giving up too much control. Teachers who think class meetings take too much time away from academic learning forget how much time they waste every day handling discipline problems that could be handled more effectively in a class meeting. We talked with a fourth-grade teacher who had all these objections. She said:

> When our school psychologist gave me a copy of *Positive Discipline* and wanted me to implement class meetings, my initial reaction was, "Oh, no. This is another program that I'm going to have to read, and it's not going to work." No one could have a more negative attitude to this than I did, but I decided to try it anyway. After one week, I was sold.

This teacher admitted that before she implemented class meetings, she was in the psychologist's office several times a week for help with her many problem students. She seldom goes to the psychologist anymore. She and her students are solving problems and helping each other.

We cannot sufficiently stress the importance of student participation in the problem-solving process to create cooperation, collaboration, positive motivation, and healthy self-esteem. How could this not improve the academic climate? Class meetings provide a solid base for the teaching, retention, and positive application of academic learning. Understanding this basic fact requires

8

an understanding of long-range results instead of short-term convenience.

## The Big Picture

All too often, school administrators and teachers do not see the big picture for young people. They overlook the crucial need for the development of life skills. They rely (often futilely) on external control instead of taking the time and energy to help students learn control from within. Teachers often choose a punishment/reward system (external controls) because they believe that it teaches children responsibility. However, this system actually makes the *teacher* responsible, not the students. It is the teacher's responsibility to catch students being *good* and reward them, or catch them being *bad* and punish them. What happens when the teacher is not around?

Another illusion perpetuated by the external-control system is that it works. It is true that punishment will usually stop misbehavior for a while, and rewards will often serve as motivators. But how many positive long-range results are there? None.

We often hear this question from teachers: "What can I do when the student has such a terrible home life?" The answer is, "A lot." Young people have several major influences in their lives: home, school, peer group, and (sometimes) church. Teachers cannot do anything directly about the home or church lives of students, but they can have a direct, positive impact on school and peer group experiences—a large portion of a student's day. The skills and attitudes learned by students have a ripple effect into the playground, the community, and the home.

Teachers do not have to feel overwhelmed by the responsibility of their power to nurture and influence students. The beauty of the class-meeting process is that teachers do not have to do it all alone. Through class meetings, students learn to help one another. Everyone benefits. Responsible citizenship requires a high degree of social interest—the desire and ability to contribute in socially useful ways and not participate in antisocial behavior. In class meetings, students solve problems together and learn the tools of mutual respect, cooperation, and collaboration. They experience positive power, and this empowerment reduces their need to act out and create discipline problems in order to feel powerful.

## Putting It All Together

Teachers who wish to replace authoritarian methods with democratic ones will focus on long-range results instead of short-term convenience. When teachers have faith in themselves and their students and are willing to believe that skills can be learned, successful class meetings will likely result. Class meetings are effective when teachers are willing to give up control *over* students in favor of gaining cooperation *with* students. Teachers who learn how to ask more questions and give fewer lectures develop a real curiosity about their students' thoughts and opinions. When kids are encouraged to express their opinions, are given choices instead of edicts, and can use group problem solving, the classroom atmosphere improves as it becomes one of cooperation, collaboration, and mutual respect. The dream can become a reality.

# CHAPTER
# 2

# The Message of Caring

We have established that the class meeting process is the foundation for positive discipline in the classroom. Unless we create an atmosphere of love and caring, the foundation is built on sand.

A group of middle school students were asked, "What usually happens when you get in trouble at school?" The kids responded with various answers, including detention, Saturday school, lunch detention, suspension, extra homework, getting yelled at, being grounded or beaten up at home, having parents come to school and sitting with them to embarrass them, or referral (which they defined as getting sent to the office to listen to a speech).

They were then asked, how many of them had experienced any of those consequences. Two out of ten had been beaten up at home for poor behavior in school. Five had had their parents come to school. Every one had served detention, been grounded, been yelled at, or received extra homework. At least seven out of ten had received lunch detention, Saturday school, and suspension. When asked if these interventions helped them do better in school, they said, "No!" in unison. When asked if these interventions helped them feel loved, cared for, and motivated to cooperate, the students laughed and replied, "What do you think?"

"Why do you think grownups do these kinds of things if they don't help?" we continued. "Because they like the power," some answered. "You don't think they do it because they care about you and want to help you do better?" The kids just laughed.

Dr. James Tunney, a former educator and NFL referee, did a study for his doctoral dissertation to measure levels of perceived caring.[1] He first surveyed principals with the question, "Do you care about your teachers?" The principals always reported high levels of caring. Dr. Tunney then surveyed the teachers and found that if they perceived extremely low levels of caring from their principals.

The next step was to ask the teachers, "Do you care about your students?" Of course, the teachers reported high levels of caring about the students. But guess what? The students perceived extremely low levels of caring from their teachers.

During in-service training, when we ask the teachers how many of them care about kids, just about every hand goes up. Then we ask how many think the kids *know* they care, and, though fewer hands are raised, most teachers still believe students are getting the message. Unfortunately, as Dr. Tunney's research shows, very few kids believe teachers care about them unless they are *A* students who

[1]James Joseph Tunney and James Mancel Jenkins, "A Comparison of Climate as Perceived by Selected Students, Faculty and Administrators in PASCL, Innovative and Other High Schools," Ph.D. diss., University of Southern California, 1975.

have "psyched out the teacher" and know how to play the teacher's game.

Kids know you care when you find out who they are, encourage them to see mistakes as opportunities to learn and grow, and have faith in their ability to make a meaningful contribution. They know you care when they feel listened to and their thoughts and feelings are taken seriously. All these things happen during class meetings, with a minimum investment in patience and time for skill building. An atmosphere of caring begins with the teacher, who guides students to treat one another in ways that demonstrate caring.

## The Power of Caring

Carter Bayton, a teacher in an inner-city New York school, expressed the idea of caring in these moving words: "You have to touch the heart before you can reach the mind." In September 1991, *Life* magazine featured a story about Bayton and seventeen second-graders who had been labeled "unteachable" in a regular classroom. He taught them so well that in six months they challenged the "regular class" (which they had been deemed unfit to enter) to a math contest—and won!

Carter Bayton understands the importance of treating students with kindness and firmness. He knows it's important to make sure the message of caring gets through. This is a truly essential part of a teacher-student relationship. We have many opportunities to convey our message of caring, and we must be sure to seize them. When students feel cared about, they want to cooperate, not misbehave. When they do not *need* to misbehave to gain attention and significance, they are free to learn. Class meetings provide a format in which students can gain attention and feel significant and productive.

## Barriers and Builders

Class meetings help create the kind of environment for empowering students to be respectful, resourceful, cooperative, and capable. It is worth the effort. Respect and encouragement are two basic ingredients of caring. We have identified five common behaviors (barriers) that adults use with young people that are disrespectful and discouraging, and five behaviors (builders) that are respectful and encouraging.[2]

### Barrier 1: Assuming

We often assume we know what students think and feel without asking them. We also assume what they can or can't do and how they should or shouldn't respond. We then deal with them according to *our* assumptions, preventing us from discovering their unique capabilities.

### Builder 1: Checking

Class meetings provide an opportunity for teachers to discover what students actually think and feel. When we check instead of assume, we discover how students are maturing in their ability to deal with problems and issues that affect them.

One special-education teacher, trained in behavior modification, assumed her students were not capable of

[2]See also H. Stephen Glenn and Jane Nelsen, *Raising Self-Reliant Children in a Self-Indulgent World* (Rocklin, CA: Prima Publishing, 1989), and *Empowering Others: Ten Keys to Affirming and Validating People,* a video with H. Stephen Glenn (Provo, UT: Sunrise Books, Tapes, and Videos, 1988).

participating in class meetings; she believed it was her job to control their behavior. She was encouraged to test her assumptions by trying a class meeting. Even though the children couldn't write their names, each had a special "mark" they could stamp on the agenda to signify they wanted help with a problem. The teacher discovered that the children were more capable than she assumed. They quickly learned to express their needs at the class meeting and engage in problem solving far beyond the teacher's assumptions.

### Barrier 2: Rescuing/Explaining

We often think we are being caring or helpful when we do things *for* students rather than allow them to have their own experiences to learn from. Likewise, we may think we're being helpful by explaining things to students, instead of letting them discover the explanation for themselves.

### Builder 2: Exploring

Class meetings enable teachers to help students learn to make choices as well as understand themselves, others, and situations through their own experiences.

Teachers explain and rescue when they say, "It's cold outside, so don't forget your jackets." Teachers explore when they say, "As you look outside, what do you need to think about before you go out to recess? What do you need to do to take care of yourselves?"

### Barrier 3: Directing

We don't realize how disrespectful we are to students when we direct them. "Pick that up!" "Put that away!" "Straighten up your desk before the bell rings!" These are all directives that reinforce dependency, eliminate initiative and cooperation, and encourage passive-aggressive behavior (grudgingly doing the minimum amount of work, leaving as much undone as possible in order to "bug" the teacher).

### Builder 3: Inviting/Encouraging

Class meetings allow teachers to involve students in the planning and problem-solving activities that can help them become self-directed. ("The bell will ring soon. I would appreciate anything any of you could do to help me get the room straightened up for the next class.") Students are motivated to cooperate when they participate in designing a solution to a problem or in organizing a project.

### Barrier 4: Expecting

It is important that teachers have high expectations for young people and believe in their potential. However, when that potential becomes the standard and we judge them for falling short, we discourage them. ("I was expecting more maturity from you. I thought you were more responsible than that. I expected you to be the kind of student your brother was.")

### Builder 4: Celebrating

Class meetings let teachers and students acknowledge each other through compliments. When we are quick to celebrate any movement in the direction of a student's potential or maturity, we encourage. When we demand too much too soon, we discourage.

A student who has never risked asking a question and suddenly asks a question unrelated to the topic being discussed, could be affirmed for asking the question instead of criticized for not paying attention. Students who cheat can be affirmed for their desire to pass, and then invited to explore other ways to accomplish their goal.

### Barrier 5: "Ism-ing"

"Adultisms" occur when we forget that children are not mature adults and expect them to think and act like adults. The language of "ism-ing" is, "How come you never . . . ?" "Why can't you ever . . . ?" "Surely you realize . . . ?" "How many times do I have to tell you?" "I can't believe you would do such a thing!" "You are such a disappointment." Almost anything that begins with *should* or *ought* is usually an "adultism." They produce guilt and shame rather than support and encouragement. The message of an "ism" is, "Since you don't see what I see, you are at fault."

### Builder 5: Respecting

Class meetings encourage interaction between teachers and students that help both understand differences in how people perceive things. This understanding creates a climate of acceptance that encourages growth and effective communication. Instead of judging people for what they don't see, we encourage them to seek understanding of themselves and others.

Instead of saying, "You knew what I wanted on this project!" a teacher could say, "What is your understanding of the requirements for this project?" or, "What were you thinking of when you presented your project this way?"

The five barriers discourage students from growing and developing into capable young people. Teachers who use the barriers usually have good intentions, believing students will be motivated by assumptions, by being rescued and directed, by expectations, and by "isms." But the barriers create frustration and discouragement for teachers

17

and students alike. Switching to the five builders empowers both teachers and students. As teachers think of students as people, it is easier to empower them by checking, exploring, inviting and encouraging, celebrating, and respecting. A teacher tells the following story:

> When I first heard about the barriers and builders, I realized that I was using barriers with my students. I assumed they needed me to step in and take care of things, explain things, direct them where to go and what to do, point out where they fell short of my expectations for the day by "shoulding" on them. Then I ended up lecturing, using expressions like "How many times must I tell you?" or "You know better than that!" I felt exhausted, and the students weren't progressing.
>
> I switched to builders. I checked the students' understanding of a problem, explored their perceptions of how to work with it, invited their assistance in finding a solution, celebrated any movement in the desired direction rather than pointing out where they fell short of my expectations, and showed respect for them by honoring their thoughts and feelings. The classroom atmosphere improved. So did my disposition and the kids' progress.

We guarantee 100% improvement in student-teacher relationships when teachers simply learn to recognize barrier behaviors and stop demonstrating them. Where else can you get such a generous return for ceasing a behavior? And when the builders are added, the payoff is even greater.

A high school principal told us that the chapter in *Raising Self-Reliant Children in a Self-Indulgent World* on barriers and builders totally changed his relationship with his twenty-two-year-old daughter, who was away at college. The next time he had a telephone conversation with her, he listened. Every time he felt tempted to use his usual barriers of expecting, assuming, lecturing, rescuing, or directing, he kept his mouth shut. His daughter opened up and told him more than she ever had before. At the end of the conversation, she said, "You sure are different, Dad." She called more often after that, and there was a warmer feeling between them. He concluded his story by saying, "You were right. I got 100% return in an improved relationship by doing nothing."

## Caring Attitudes and Skills

In addition to the barriers and builders, there are attitude changes teachers can make and skills they can learn that will demonstrate to students that their teachers really care about them.

### *Awareness of Tone of Voice*

Many teachers are completely unaware of their tone of voice and how it can affect students. In one junior high school class, for example, the students were in serious conflict with their teacher, who couldn't understand their hostility. A visitor to the classroom was shocked to watch the teacher's manner and listen to her tone of voice. Whenever students misbehaved, she yelled at them, criticized them, and humiliated them in front of their classmates. After class, the visitor asked the teacher if she would like some feedback. She said yes and was told, "You are trying to put out a small fire with a blowtorch." Having been completely unaware of her manner and tone, the teacher changed both by the next class period. That same day she told another faculty member, "My classes have been much smoother this afternoon since I decided to put away my blowtorch."

19

## Listening and Taking Kids Seriously

A seventeen-year-old high school student decided not to turn in any of his homework, in order to punish his teacher for her "attitude problem." Whenever he tried to talk to her about homework, he thought she was insinuating that he was lazy and didn't take him seriously. He did well on the tests, and thought the teacher was picking on him *because* he didn't turn his work in.

With encouragement from his parents, he decided to talk to his teacher about his feelings. This time, she really listened. When he finished, she said, "I know it seems unfair that I insist on homework regardless of how well you do on a test. I'm sorry this upsets you, but I'm unwilling to change the rule. I thought you didn't care about school, and I apologize for treating you disrespectfully. I'm glad you took the time to tell me how you feel." Although the conversation didn't change the homework situation, the young man felt understood and accepted, and he stopped acting out in the classroom.

## Enjoying the Job

Robert Rasmussen, called Ras by his students, was voted High School Teacher of the Year five years in a row by juniors and seniors. The school district also honored him as Teacher of the Year.

While Ras was out of the room, we asked the students why they thought Ras received these honors. Their answers could be divided into three categories: He respects us, he listens to us, and he enjoys his job. "What does enjoying the job have to do with anything?" we asked. One of the students explained, "Many teachers come to work with an attitude problem. They hate us. They hate their jobs. They seem to hate life. They take it out on us. Ras is always up. He seems to enjoy us, his job, and life in general."

Ras has a unique way of making sure the message of caring gets through. He has a teddy bear in his classroom. He introduces the bear to his students and says, "This is our care bear. If any of you feels discouraged or a little down, come get the bear. He'll make you feel better." At first the students think he's bonkers. After all, they are high school juniors and seniors, young adults. But it doesn't take long for them to catch the spirit. Every day, several students, including the big football players, go to Ras's desk and say, "Give me the bear."

The bear concept became so popular that Ras had to provide more bears to keep up with the demand. Sometimes the kids carry them around all day, but they always bring them back. Sometimes, when Ras sees a student who looks a little down, he tosses a bear to the student. This is his symbolic way of saying, "I care. I don't have time to spend with you personally right now, but I care."

## *Appreciating Uniqueness*

A student thinks a teacher cares when his or her uniqueness is recognized. One teacher made a set of baseball cards for his third-grade class, with each card having a student's picture and nickname. The nicknames expressed the unique interest of each child. For example, one card said "Cat-Lover Colleen" and another, "Home-Run Sean." Although it takes time and skill to make a set of baseball cards, it can be fun to let the kids come up with nicknames together, as long as the activity remains respectful.

Another way of expressing each students' uniqueness is to have them create their own T-shirts. Give each student a piece of paper cut out in the form of a T-shirt, with the following instructions:

1. Write your name at the top of the shirt.
2. In the middle, write one word that describes you.

21

3. Write words that describe some of your characteristics and special interests all over the shirt.

4. Across the bottom, write one thing about you that most people probably don't know.

5. Tape the T-shirt on your clothes with masking tape, and walk around the room. Talk to at least three other people using the information on your T-shirt as the basis of conversation.

## Developing an Appropriate Attitude

Think about how you feel when you're watching babies and toddlers; it seems like everything they do is adorable. See if you can get to the point with your students where you can truly say, "Aren't they cute!"

When we are able to see behavior as age-appropriate, it helps us see otherwise annoying behavior as cute. A third-grade boy in torn, dirty pants will begin to look adorable, a seventh-grader acting like a "big shot" will bring a smile, and a teacher might even look forward to hearing the latest installment from a high school student who "knows much more than you."

## Having a Sense of Humor

Sometimes teachers forget to see the humor in situations with students. It's okay not to be serious all the time. Mrs. Turner plays a game with her class called Let's Make a Deal, and the kids love it. She says, "Okay, kids, it's time for Let's Make a Deal. I like to start on time, and you like to leave on time. I'll save up the time I have to wait to get started, and you can make it up after school. Deal?" The kids groan and then settle down.

Mr. Barkley has a droll sense of humor that kids love. They know he cares about them and whether or not they succeed in school. Some teachers use sarcasm in the guise of humor to put students down, and others may "go for a laugh" at a student's expense. With Mr. Barkley, the students sense the feeling behind what he does, and his caring comes through. If there is sincere caring for the kids, they will get the message.

One day, Mr. Barkley was dealing with a daydreaming student. He put his hand lightly on the boy's shoulder and said, "Picture this. You're eighteen years old. You get up and turn on MTV. You know everyone on the videos and all the words to the songs. But will anyone give you a job? No way! And why not? Because you spent all your time in my class staring into space." The student looked up, grinned, and opened his book.

Later in the period, a student, Jennifer, was passing notes to a friend and paying no attention to a play Mr. Barkley was reading to the class. In a smooth but slightly louder voice, Mr. Barkley read, "To be or not to be, that is the question Jennifer asks herself each day." She looked up and said, "Huh? Were you calling on me?" Mr. Barkley said, "Did anyone hear me call on Jennifer? I don't think so." Jennifer paid attention to the rest of class.

## Respecting Students' Outside Interests

It's easy to forget that students have other interests in life besides school. Their social life is extremely important to them, and often they are dealing with rejection or popularity. They may be dealing with the trauma of not being chosen for teams, or never being the first or the best. By the time they reach junior high and high school, they may have (among others) job issues, car issues, dating issues, sex issues, and drug issues.

Many kids operate according to a different clock than adults do. They like to stay up late and then have difficulty getting up in the morning. Yet they have to conform to an early start at school. We saw this note pasted on a door of a high school classroom in Charlotte, North Carolina:

> Tardies, please come into the room quietly, find a seat, look for your directions on the board. Learning begins as soon as the tardy bell rings.

Instead of humiliating or punishing latecomers, this teacher respectfully allows students to experience the consequences and take care of what they need to do to catch up. Students can come in and start working right away instead of going to the office, getting papers, feeling like they're in trouble, and disturbing the class.

Another teacher tells his students, "I won't take roll until five minutes after the tardy bell. I know some of you have jobs and have a difficult time handling all the demands of teenagers. It would be better if you could sleep in until 10:00, go to school until 5:00, and have the rest of the evening for family time, jobs, and a social life." The kids cheer. They do their best not to take advantage. They respect this teacher because *they* feel respected. He knows how to make sure the message of caring get through.

### Involving Students

Many teachers are used to directing students and trying to solve student problems themselves. Then they wonder why students resist. We have been in many classrooms where the teacher's neatly printed "Classroom Rules" are posted on the wall. With this method, students become *passive recipients* of a teacher's demands—what an invitation for them to either give in or rebel.

Some teachers have found a way to invite cooperation. They wait until the first day of school and ask the kids to be involved in brainstorming classroom rules. Their list of ideas is quickly scribbled on paper, labeled "Our

Rules," and posted on the wall. This is an invitation for kids to cooperate, because they have participated in the decisions. What is surprising is that the rules are the same as, or stricter than, the rules teachers try to force on students.

Students feel a teacher's caring when they are consulted and involved. They rise to the occasion when a teacher says, "This is our learning environment, and together we are responsible for making it work." Teachers who fear a loss of control if they allow that kind of student input will be delighted to find that control is not needed. Cooperation and collaboration, based on mutual respect, replace control.

### Improvement, Not Perfection

Students know a teacher cares when the teacher encourages improvement instead of insisting on perfection. The class-meeting process provides an excellent opportunity for students to trust this philosophy. Class meetings may never be perfect, but every failure can provide an opportunity for solutions. The teacher should continue asking, "What can we do to solve this problem?" Not only does this question show teachers care, it encourages kids to care about each other.

## Caring in Class Meetings

The power of caring through class meetings is demonstrated in the following examples. Frank Meder, a teacher in the Sacramento City School District, started class meetings in a school where violence in the elementary school was so bad that the janitor periodically had to clean up blood. Vandalism was so prevalent that the sheriff was called on a weekly basis. Frank said that he got a stomach ache every Sunday afternoon around 1:00 because he dreaded returning to the classroom Monday morning. When Frank decided to try class meetings, he felt more desperate than hopeful. He doubted that his disruptive students could learn cooperation and problem-solving skills; he was delighted to be proven wrong. The year Frank started class meetings, it came to the attention of his principal that although there were sixty-one suspensions for fights, not one student was from Frank's class. She also noticed that Frank's students came to school more regularly and were improving academically. When the principal sat in on one of Frank's class meetings, she realized what a great preventive tool the meeting was and asked Frank to show all the teachers in the school how to conduct class meetings.

The following year, every teacher, first through sixth grade, had class meetings at least four times a week. The following statistics were reported by Ann Platt in her master's thesis at California State University, Sacramento: only four suspensions for fighting as opposed to sixty-one the year before; only two cases of reported vandalism, as opposed to twenty-four the year before.[3]

In another instance, a school with a serious graffiti problem kept hiring painters to repaint the walls. Every time a wall was repainted, the kids put graffiti on it again. One of the teachers suggested asking the student body for ideas on how to solve the problem. The students decreed that when kids were caught writing on the wall, they would be supervised by another student monitor while they repainted. It's no surprise that the graffiti problem disappeared.

[3]Ann Roeder Platt, "Efficacy of Class Meetings in Elementary Schools," project submitted in partial satisfaction of the requirements for the degree of Master of Science in Counseling, California State University, 1979.

Another example of the power of caring through a class meeting is provided by Earl Lesk.[4] Mr. Lesk, a high school teacher, decided to initiate regular class meetings in his Biology 11 and 12 classes. He asked his students if they would like to participate, and they said yes. One eleventh-grade student, who'd had difficulty in all aspects of the course, but finished the semester successfully, summed up the class feelings: "By using encouragement and not forcing people to do things, the class became more independent and cooperative, which allowed us to use our own initiative to put forth a good effort."

These teachers and schools have incorporated class meetings with excellent results. They are just a few of the many who have experienced tremendous success by starting class meetings. If a teacher is willing to learn a process that teaches students many valuable skills, it can also make the job easier and more fun. Helping students experience caring, belonging, and significance is the most powerful thing a teacher can do, motivating them to fulfill their highest potential—academically and otherwise.

Effective class meetings help students become more self-confident. They help improve self-esteem by increasing a sense of belonging and self-acceptance. As students contribute to the meeting, they find that they have the ability to make a difference and feel a sense of ownership through participation. They soon understand that teachers care about them and their concerns, and that their contributions are valued.

[4]Earl Lesk, "Freedom with Responsibility," *The B. C. Teacher,* January/February 1982.

## CHAPTER
# 3

# Building Blocks for Effective Class Meetings

**T**here are many types of student-teacher meetings. Positive discipline class meetings are not designed to be used once in a while to solve a crisis. Without regularly scheduled class meetings, students don't develop the skills for success in solving a problem. Positive discipline class meetings are not the kind of meetings where the teacher determines the topics to be discussed and does most of the talking (preaching, lecturing) in an effort to manipulate students into good behavior. Students usually resist and tune out teacher-dominated meetings.

The positive discipline class meeting is a process that involves teachers and students in true dialogue and problem solving on issues of real and practical concern to them. Most of the agenda items are student-initiated, although we suggest teachers also put *their* concerns on the agenda, so that students can help solve some of the teacher's problems. When students and teachers collaborate, they learn to appreciate each other, to understand and respect differences, and to develop social interest.

## Feedback and Training

After hearing about the many benefits of class meetings, many teachers try them, only to be discouraged by poor results. If you are one of those teachers, we encourage you to read the entire book before you decide, "Never again." You may discover the reasons for previous problems.

A fourth-grade teacher was struggling with a group of students who had driven previous teachers to tranquilizers and fantasies of early retirement. He hoped class meetings would be the way to teach his students cooperation and responsibility. After trying and failing, he discovered that holding class meetings once a week with the students remaining in rows at their desks was the problem. Shortly after he started holding the meetings in a circle format for twenty minutes every day, his class changed dramatically.

After receiving training in positive discipline in the classroom, some teachers discover they had been patronizing, punitive, controlling, or had allowed humiliation to take place in their classes. Class meetings will not be successful under these conditions. Many teachers discovered that making some small change in what they were doing was enough to bring a positive atmosphere to their class-meeting process. We would like to present three of their most important discoveries, all of which are discussed in more detail in later chapters.

1. Focus on solutions instead of consequences. Too many students and teachers still use punishment, and focusing on solutions helps eliminate this problem.

2. Allow the student who put the problem on the agenda to choose the solution he or she thinks will be helpful instead of allowing the students to vote. This increases the feeling of empowerment and accountability for that student.

3. Be patient and take time for training while both you and your students learn the class-meeting process—often through mistakes.

We stress repeatedly that it takes time for teachers and students to give up control and punishment and to become comfortable with new methods. Most of us are willing to take the time for training when we see the value of new methods.

## Eight Building Blocks

Training in the Eight Building Blocks for effective class meetings is the surest route to success. Proficiency in these building-block skill areas will produce meetings in which kids want to become involved in the problem-solving process. It takes about two hours to introduce these concepts to students, and we recommend that you hold short sessions and take at least four class meetings to cover the basics, which are discussed in this book over the course of Chapters 3 through 7. Let your students know that you are taking extra time up front to lay the groundwork for successful class meetings. If the topics are introduced gradually, students will be less restless and will have a chance to practice the skills they have learned. The Eight Building Blocks are listed below.

1. Forming a circle.

2. Practicing compliments and appreciation.

3. Creating an agenda.

4. Developing communication skills.

5. Learning about separate realities.

6. Solving problems through role playing and brainstorming.

7. Recognizing the four reasons people do what they do.

8. Applying logical consequences and other non-punitive solutions.

## Getting Agreement First

Before forming your first circle and beginning to introduce the Eight Building Blocks to your class, take time to introduce the idea of class meetings to your students and get their "buy-in." We have found the following discussions work well with various age groups.

Introduce your students to the idea that you would like to begin holding class meetings where they can express their concerns and use their power and skills to help make decisions. Elementary students are usually eager to try class meetings. Simply ask for a show of hands of how many students would like to begin. When teachers use the attitudes and skills we have discussed, elementary students rarely resist.

With junior high and high school students, however, it is helpful to get them to buy in to the idea of class meetings before starting. Otherwise, they may resist and will probably sabotage the process. Using language appropriate for your grade level, initiate a discussion about power. Talk to them about how problems are usually handled in their school (with punishment and reward). Point out how that method creates a one-up/one-down system in which adults tell kids what to do and kids either comply or rebel without thinking or becoming involved.

It is a win/lose system. None of us want to be the losers, so we need to create a win/win system.

To encourage discussion, ask questions like these: "Who has an example they would like to share about what happens when someone tries to control you? What do you feel? What do you do? What do you learn? How do you try to control or manipulate others, including teachers?" Kids will usually say that they feel angry or scared and manipulated. What they learn is to rebel or comply.

Ask them if they would like to be more involved in the decisions that affect their lives. Would they be willing to do the work required to come up with win/win solutions? Point out that some students actually *prefer* having adults boss them around, so that they can rebel. Other students like having adults direct them, so they don't have to take responsibility themselves. It takes more time and personal responsibility from everyone to use class meetings effectively. Make it clear that you don't intend to waste time teaching and learning a respectful method if they prefer continuing with the usual disrespectful method in which the teacher has control and a student's only options are to comply, rebel, and/or spend time in detention. This kind of discussion is especially helpful and effective in classrooms where students have been taught with authoritarian methods.

Another possibility is to start a discussion by asking your students how many have family meetings at home. Ask what happens at family meetings. Let them know that class meetings are a place where they can help each other, share ideas, solve problems, and plan things together. Mention that while it's okay to discuss anything at a class meeting, there may be some items that can't be changed, like curriculum or school policies. Nevertheless, if someone has a concern about these matters, it can be discussed with the intention of determining the best way to deal with things that can't be changed.

Once you have the interest and go-ahead of your students, establish how often you will be holding class meetings, so that everyone will know ahead of time. Some teachers prefer a half-hour meeting once a week. Others take ten to thirty minutes each day or three times a week. In the beginning, it may be important to have a class meeting every day while students are learning the Eight Building Blocks. If meetings are held only once a week, younger students might be discouraged from putting something on an agenda that already has ten items. Because they know only three or four topics can be covered in a single meeting, they may be frustrated at having to wait three to four weeks before their concerns gets addressed. Once a week may be enough for older students and students with strong problem-solving skills. Many teachers find the process so valuable for teaching cooperation and life skills that they hold class meetings daily. These teachers find academic learning is enhanced in spite of the time taken away from academics. The important thing is to decide what works best for you, then stick to the schedule you set. Introduce your students to the format for class meetings so they know what will happen in the meeting once they learn the eight building blocks. In Chapter 7, we explain each part of the format in detail. At this time, your purpose is to simply give the students an overview of what will happen at a class meeting.

### Class Meeting Format

1. Compliments and appreciations.
2. Follow-up on prior solutions.
3. Agenda items.
   a. Share feelings while others listen.
   b. Discuss without fixing.
   c. Ask for problem-solving help.
4. Future plans (field trips, parties, projects).

We recommend you teach the Eight Building Blocks while students are in the circle. You are beginning a new tradition and setting up a different way of relating to each other.

## ▼ *Building Block 1: Forming a Circle*

Tell students that the first step in the class meeting is to create an atmosphere where win/win solutions can take place and where everyone has an equal right to speak and be heard. A circle arrangement—without any tables or desks—allows everyone to see everyone else, and it will remind students that the class meeting is a different and special part of their experience at school.

Ask the kids for suggestions about how to arrange the circle with the least amount of chaos. Really listen to their ideas and review their proposals instead of telling them what to do. They love seeing their ideas written on the board. When they think they have a plan that will work, they're ready to move the furniture. If possible, find a student with a stopwatch to time the class (or use a clock). Let the kids get started without any instruction from you.

If you are willing to be flexible instead of thinking there is only one way, each class could end up with a different arrangement. For example, one class we heard about formed a square with the tables, and students on top of the tables. Another class stacked all the tables in the corner and made a circle with the chairs. Another class pushed the tables and chairs to the back of the room and sat in a circle on the floor. Let the kids be creative. If their first try doesn't work, discuss it, and let them come up with some new possibilities.

After all the furniture is moved, write on the board how long it took. Ask the kids if they have any ideas for improvement. Encourage them to discuss the process.

Without realizing it, the kids are having their first discussion that will set the tone for future meetings. They are learning by doing, not by being lectured at; you are showing and allowing them to be involved. Ask them if they would like to put the room back to normal and try again, to see if they can cut down on the time. Sit back and enjoy observing how much kids can learn from doing something, discussing it, and trying again.

Each person in the classroom needs a chair in the circle. If anyone is left out, ask the students to scoot backward to make room. Some teachers prefer to make a seating chart, assigning seats in the circle. This style decision is up to you. It is important, however, that all students, classroom aides, and the teacher are in the circle before continuing. If the class decides to sit in a circle on the floor, the teacher must be seated at the same level and in the circle with the students.

## ▼ Building Block 2: Practicing Compliments and Appreciations

It's important to start the class meeting on a positive note, and it's a real boost to everyone's self-esteem when students and teachers say nice things to one another. Since most kids aren't used to giving compliments, we suggest using the first class meeting to teach them how. One way is asking them to think of a time when someone said something that made them feel good about themselves. They can take turns sharing their examples with the group.

Another suggestion is asking your students to think about something they would like to thank others for. Give examples. Perhaps they would like to thank a classmate for making a poster or lending a pencil. Maybe they would want to thank someone for playing catch or jacks with them. They might like to thank someone for walking to the playground with them or for being a friend by eating lunch with them. It doesn't take many examples before the kids get the idea and can think of something they appreciate.

Another way to teach compliments is to ask the kids to think of something they wish someone would compliment *them* on. Then ask if someone in the class would like to give that compliment to the person who suggested it. For instance, Whitney might wish someone would compliment her on how hard she is trying not to talk out of turn. She tells this to the class. Zack, one of her classmates, says to Whitney, "I would like to compliment you on how well you are doing not talking out of turn." Whitney should respond with, "Thank you." You would then ask Zack if he has something he would like to be complimented on, and continue the procedure.

You can also teach compliments by asking your students, "What do grown-ups usually do when they get a compliment?" Emphasize that it's hard even for grown-ups to give and receive compliments, because compliments often don't focus on what someone does. If we focus on what someone does, others will get a better idea of what we like. For instance, a student might say, "I want to compliment you for letting us have class meetings," which is much more informed than simply saying, "You're a nice teacher."

Students can also learn to make their compliments and appreciations specific. If someone says "You're nice," you can help the student be more specific by suggesting saying, "You're nice because . . . " Or ask the student to give an example of something the person did that he or she thought was nice.

If students are having a hard time coming up with compliments, remind them how easy it would be if they were asked to think of criticisms and put-downs instead. One teacher said to his class, "Isn't it a shame how easy it is for us to be negative and how hard it is for us to be positive? Wouldn't it be nicer if we had more positives in our lives? Let's keep practicing until this gets easier."

It helps to give students examples of statements that might seem like compliments at first, but that aren't really very encouraging. These are called "back-handed" compliments. You can ask the students, "What's wrong with this compliment?" and then give an example, such as "I'm glad you like me better than the rest of the kids." "I'd like to compliment you for sharing your candy with me, because usually you are very selfish."

If someone gives a compliment that is really a criticism, ask, "How many people think what Sandra said is a compliment? Raise your hands. How many people do not?" Then ask Sandra if she would like to try again or ask for help to turn the criticism into a compliment. If Sandra can't think of a way to change her statement, ask for suggestions from the class. This models the *helping* rather than the hurting principle. It is also okay for students to pass, but it is important not to let a criticism slide by without addressing it.

Spend some time on how to receive a compliment. We recommend that people acknowledge compliments with a simple "Thank you," so the person who gave the compliment knows it was heard. Once students understand how to give a compliment, help them take turns by using an item—such as a bean bag or pencil—that can be passed around. Send the item around the circle with these instructions: "When you're holding the item in your hand, you can either give a compliment, tell someone what you would like to be complimented on, or pass." This poster idea shown in Figure 3.1 can serve as a reminder and add a sense of fun.

At first, the kids may feel uncomfortable or think giving compliments is silly. If you stick with the activity so they can practice, the skills will grow, and so will the good

---

**Two,
four,
six,
eight.
What do we appreciate?
Compliments,
Appreciations,
Acknowledgments.**

---

Figure 3.1

feelings in the classroom. Many teachers who have class meetings regularly tell us that students complain when a meeting is called off because nothing is on the agenda. They say, "Well, we could at least do compliments."

Giving compliments may be threatening to junior high school students. They seem to find the words *appreciations* and *acknowledgments* easier to use than the word *compliments*. Ask questions to warm them up. For instance, you might ask the students to tell about something that really makes them angry, to talk about some activity they like to do, or to share their favorite food or music. Such topics are nonthreatening, and they give students an opportunity to break through barriers and get to know one another better.

## ▼ Building Block 3: Creating an Agenda

Let your students know that you will set up a notebook for agenda items. Students and teachers can put concerns on the agenda during the day. It may become disruptive when students congregate and linger around the agenda book. To avoid this kind of disturbance, have the kids determine specific agenda-setting times, such as just before leaving the room for recess or lunch.

The only items that will be handled at the class meeting are those that are in the agenda book before the meeting. Between meetings, remember to put items on the agenda, instead of trying to solve problems yourself right when they occur. If a student comes to you complaining about another person in the class, say, "That's something we can talk about at the class meeting. Would you please add it to the agenda?" Some teachers take dictation from students who are too young to write. This approach serves two functions. It saves you time (you don't have to deal with every problem), and it gives the students real problems to solve at the class meeting.

Many teachers want to start problem solving right away. We strongly suggest you wait until you have taught all of the eight building blocks before dealing with items on the agenda. Encourage your students to start putting concerns on the agenda so you will have things to work on as soon as they learn the skills.

Forming a circle, reviewing the meeting's purpose and format, including establishing the agenda, and learning about compliments are plenty of topics for the first meeting. Let your students know when the next meeting will be, tell them where the agenda book will be kept, and have them return the furniture to the normal arrangement.

## CHAPTER
# 4

# Strengthening Communication Skills

Communication skills, such as being a good listener, taking turns, expressing oneself clearly, and respecting separate realities, may be introduced at the second class meeting after forming the circle and delivering compliments. The most effective way to teach skills is through experiential activities that help students discover what works and what doesn't work.

## Experiential Activities

The most effective way to introduce activities is to follow these four steps:

1. Explain the activity.
2. Demonstrate the activity with a volunteer student.
3. Let the kids try the activity.

4. Allow them to process their responses by expressing their thoughts and feelings.

Although these steps may not be appropriate for every
activity, we have found there is less confusion if students
first hear about it, then see it demonstrated, and then try
the activity themselves.

It is important to allow students to process their
responses to the activity by sharing their thoughts and feelings. The main points *you* would like to make are usually
made by the students when they express themselves. Help
the process by asking, "What were you deciding about
yourself, about the other person, or about what you are
going to do?" The answers to these questions provide a
wealth of information about the long-range effectiveness
certain behaviors have on students. For example, some
students may say that they are feeling hurt or angry and
are deciding to either "get even" or withdraw in the future.

## ▼ Building Block 4: Developing Communication Skills

You may choose any or all of the following activities to
teach listening skills. You may even want to create some
of your own.

**Activity:** Have all the kids talk at the same time. Ask how
many of them felt heard. A lively discussion may result
when you ask them to express what they were feeling,
thinking, or deciding.

**Activity:** Ask for a volunteer to share an interesting experience. Have all the other kids wave their hands in the
air to indicate they want to speak. Ask how many of them
would find this distracting while they are talking.

**Activity:** Have each student pick a partner. One student tells the other about a favorite TV show, while the other refuses to make eye contact. Then have one partner actually get up and walk away while the other is talking. Invite kids to share their thoughts, feelings, and decisions based on their experience.

As students express what they are learning from these activities, you will find that everyone is getting the message about poor listening skills. Whenever they aren't using good listening skills during class meetings, you can ask, "How many of you think we're practicing good listening skills? How many do not?" Kids can show their answers by raising their hands. Usually nothing more needs to be said in order for the problem to correct itself.

### Taking Turns

Suggest to the kids that one way to avoid the problems generated by poor listening at a class meeting is to take turns going around the circle during a discussion. It is effective to use an object that can be passed from student to student, such as a bean bag, a toy microphone, or a pencil.

When a student has the object, he or she can either make a comment, give a suggestion, or pass. It is empowering for quiet or shy students to have something tangible symbolizing personal power and the option to take a turn if they choose.

Some students need more guidance than others in the beginning. Guidance can be in the form of questions: "How many of you think it's important that we take turns so everyone is listened to with respect?" "How many of you would like a whole room of people who can help each other with problems?" "How many of you think we can find solutions to problems instead of using punishment and humiliation?" The fact that they are asked instead of told, and have an opportunity to raise their hands to show agreement, gives them a sense of inclusion and ownership.

### "I" Statements

Part of good communication is to use "I" statements. Have the kids practice "I" statements by thinking of a time when they were very happy. Have them fill in the blanks to the following: "I felt *happy* because _____ , and I wish _____ ." Then have them think of a time when they were angry, and do the same.

Feelings can usually be expressed in one word. You may wish to ask the kids to develop a list of feelings such as happy, angry, embarrassed, sad, excited, and so on, and take the time to practice "I" statements and words that express feelings.

Once kids learn the skill of using "I" statements, they have a reference point when communication breaks down. For instance, if you think someone is communicating in a blaming or judgmental way, you might ask the class, "How many think it would help if Sally used an "I" statement right now?" (Show of hands.) "Sally, would you be willing to try again using an 'I' statement? Thank you."

### Solutions, Not Blame

Introduce the concept of focusing on solutions instead of blame. Guide a discussion about this important point: If you are looking for blame, what will you find? (Blame.) Once you establish blame, then what? (You can focus on blame forever and not make any changes.) If you look for solutions, what will you find? (Solutions.) Which direction is the most productive, focusing on blame or on solutions? (Obviously, solutions.) Ask for a volunteer to make a poster like that in Figure 4.1 to hang in the room.

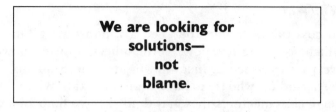

We are looking for
solutions—
not
blame.

Figure 4.1

## *Respect*

Stress the importance of avoiding humiliation and judgment to create an atmosphere of respect. Give the kids a chance to talk about times when they felt hurt or criticized, so that the class has some examples of disrespectful behavior. You might want to start the discussion by sharing some experiences of your own. At the end of the discussion, ask for volunteers to make two more posters (See Figures 4.2 and 4.3.)

We're here
to help each other
not
hurt each other.

Figure 4.2

Mutual Respect
Practiced
Here.

Figure 4.3

### Win/Win

Discuss the difference between a win/lose situation, in which someone has power over others, and the power everyone experiences in a win/win situation. Students are used to adults who try to have power over kids. When they begin class meetings, they may think this is a time for kids to have power over adults. Instead, let the kids know that for the class meeting to be a safe place, everyone must work together to find win/win ideas. A poster like the following could be a good reminder.

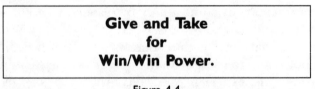

**Give and Take**
**for**
**Win/Win Power.**

Figure 4.4

### We Decided

Some classes like to make a list of guidelines for creating respectful class meetings. (Notice we use the word *guidelines,* not *rules.*) Ask students to brainstorm suggestions about what they need from each other to feel safe. Write all their ideas on the blackboard. Ask them to choose the three or five suggestions they think are the most important. Ask for a volunteer to make a "We Decided" poster, and print the three to five suggestions on the poster. It might look like this:

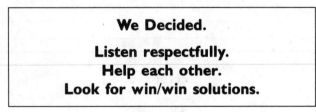

**We Decided.**

**Listen respectfully.**
**Help each other.**
**Look for win/win solutions.**

Figure 4.5

46

## ▼ Building Block 5:
## Learning About Separate Realities

Tell your students you would like to play a game that helps people understand that not everyone is the same or thinks the same way. Ask, "How many of you sometimes think there is always a right or wrong answer? How many think there's only one way to see things? How many sometimes feel embarrassed to raise your hand, because you think everyone knows the answer but you? We're going to experiment with an activity that will demonstrate that there are *at least* four different ways to look at things."

**Activity:** Collect pictures of a lion, an eagle, a turtle, and a chameleon. (Some teachers have stuffed animals, or just write the animal names on a large piece of paper.) Ask the kids, "If you could be one of these animals for one day, which one would you like to be?"

Once the students have made their decisions, have them divide up into four groups, one for each animal. Ask someone from each group to list all the characteristics the group members like about their animal at the top of a large piece of paper. At the bottom, have them list the other animals and all the reasons they *didn't* choose to be that animal. Show them the following example of how their sheets can be organized.

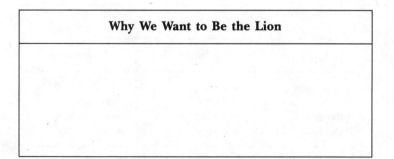

| Why We Want to Be the Lion |
|---|
|  |

| Why We Didn't Choose | | |
|---|---|---|
| **Eagle** | **Turtle** | **Chameleon** |
|  |  |  |

Below are some responses from several high school classes, in case you need to help the students with further hints or instructions.

| Why We Want to Be the Lion | | |
|---|---|---|
| king of the jungle<br>playful<br>proud<br>warm<br>takes care of<br>  personal needs | independent<br>respected<br>sociable<br>good looking | strong<br>people respond to<br>  the roar<br>passionate |
| **Why We Didn't Choose** | | |
| **Eagle** | **Turtle** | **Chameleon** |
| bird of prey<br>violent<br>endangered<br>flighty | plodding<br>vulnerable<br>avoiding<br>too slow | changes to fit in<br>insincere<br>cold blooded<br>not centered |

| Why We Want to Be the Eagle | | |
|---|---|---|
| observe | protected | gentle |
| fly | beautiful | symbol of great |
| soar | faithful | country |
| freedom | aware | independent |
| strength | respected by | keen eyes |
| long living | Indians | masters |
| control of destiny | in charge | |
| great view | intelligent | |

| Why We Didn't Choose | | |
|---|---|---|
| **Turtle** | **Chameleon** | **Lion** |
| slow | too changeable | dangerous |
| hard shell | run from prob- | hot, dry, arid |
| hide | lems | aggressive |
| weak | blend in too | lazy |
| bottom of | much | loud |
| totem pole | | macho |
| not attractive | | |

| Why We Want to Be the Turtle | | |
|---|---|---|
| sturdy | long-lived | relaxed |
| protected | cool environment | lay eggs and go |
| wise | enduring | persistent |
| gentle | steady | independent |
| can hide from | predictable | calm |
| danger | reliable | symbolize earth |
| look at details | peaceful | lay in sun |
| patient | friendly | |
| don't hurt anyone | don't bother | |
| know how to enjoy | anyone | |
| selves | trusting | |

| Why We Didn't Choose | | |
| --- | --- | --- |
| **Lion** | **Eagle** | **Chameleon** |
| fierce<br>gruesome<br>violent<br>destructive<br>arrogant "kings"<br>ruthless<br>lazy<br>predatory<br>loud<br>cunning<br>hunted | power hungry<br>loners | moody<br>volatile<br>phony<br>unreliable<br>inconsistent<br>not very strong<br>sneaky<br>unpredictable |

| Why We Want to Be the Chameleon | | |
| --- | --- | --- |
| changeable<br>unusual<br>adaptable<br>observer | passive<br>accommodating<br>listener<br>cute | harmless<br>understanding<br>flexible<br>sensitive |
| **Why We Didn't Choose** | | |
| **Lion** | **Eagle** | **Turtle** |
| loud<br>power hungry<br>meat eater<br>aggressive<br>lazy | superior<br>unapproachable<br>unadaptable | avoid<br>bite<br>slow<br>defenses |

Hang the papers on a wall next to each other. Starting with the lion, say, "These are the reasons some of our classmates decided it would be good to be a lion." Read the list. Then go to the bottom of the chameleon's list and read out loud all the reasons a chameleon wouldn't think it's a good idea to be a lion. Continue reading the eagle's reasons and the turtle's reasons for not choosing the lion. Repeat the procedure with the next animal, reading all the positive characteristics and then all the negatives before moving to the next animal.

After reading all the lists, continue the discussion by reminding the kids that everyone sees the world in a different way. Sometimes we see some things the same, just like some of us wanted to be more than one animal for different reasons. Point out that any quality can be positive or negative, and that there is no one right way to be.

Ask the students what the advantages might be if a classroom had some of each of the animals represented. What might some of the disadvantages be? How can this information be helpful at a class meeting? This activity usually generates a lot of laughs and a lively discussion.

Ask how a turtle would feel if he thought an eagle was picking on him. What would a chameleon do if he got scared by a lion? Would a lion need to stop roaring if she wanted to make friends with an eagle?

Once your students have learned the communication skills outlined in this chapter, they will know how to create an atmosphere of respect that guarantees effective class meetings. In the next chapter, they will practice role playing and brainstorming as methods of solving problems.

# CHAPTER
# 5

# Effective
# Problem-Solving Skills

**M**any of the skills children need to be successful, happy, contributing members of society are learned through problem solving. Effective problem-solving skills help students understand their role of responsibility within the classroom or any system. Problem solving helps them think, speak, and interact thoughtfully with others. They will take these skills with them into all aspects of their lives.

## ▼ *Building Block 6: Solving Problems Through Role Playing and Brainstorming*

By the third class meeting, students are usually ready to learn effective problem-solving skills. Form the circle, exchange compliments, and then tell the class that today they will be learning two new skills that will help them solve problems: role playing and brainstorming. Choose an item from the agenda that you think provides opportunities for practicing these skills. (Once students have learned class meeting skills, you will discuss agenda items in chronological order.) Remind them that today, learning the skills is more important than solving the problem.

## Simple Discussion

Sometimes role playing and brainstorming are not necessary for solving a problem. Do not underestimate the value of a simple discussion. Sometimes a discussion is enough to resolve issues on the agenda. By discussing an issue, kids get a chance to voice their opinion, share their feelings, and give suggestions. Their suggestions can be both amusing and irritating—often they say the same things you have said, which went in one ear and out the other. You can choose to feel frustrated and discounted, or be grateful that the kids listen to each other and come to your conclusions.

Often a discussion can be enough to help kids become aware of the need to make changes. At other times, it is easier to succeed at problem solving by incorporating brainstorming and/or role playing. It's also more fun. Let's start by looking at role playing.

## Role Playing

After picking the agenda item, invite the student who put the problem on the agenda to help you set up a role-play. Ask how many kids have ever role-played before. Point out that role playing is like putting on a play where class members will pretend to be different people involved in the problem they want to solve.

It's fun to play a guessing game with the students to see if they can guess the two guidelines for role playing.

Say, "I have two important guidelines for role playing in my mind. If you can guess exactly what they are, I'll give you a dollar." They'll make all kinds of guesses, such as you have to listen, you have to take turns, you have to do what the teachers says, you have to use a soft voice. Then you say, "Those are good ideas, but the two guidelines I have in my mind are: (1) You have to exaggerate, and (2) you have to have fun."

Kids almost never guess there could be a "rule" that you have to have fun. In the guessing process, not only do the kids become engaged, but you get to learn more about what they think. Explain exaggeration to the students. Give them permission not to worry about playing a part perfectly, explaining that everyone will learn more if the players exaggerate the behaviors as a way of speeding up the demonstration of life experiences. Remind them that the role-play is an opportunity to learn and help each other—it is *not* a test of perfection.

Have the student who put the issue on the agenda describe a recent occurrence of the problem. Tell him or her to describe the episode in enough detail so that the class will know how to role-play the different parts. If the story does not include enough detail, ask some of the following questions: "What happened? Then what happened? What did you do? What did the other person do? What did you say? What did the other person say?"

After the problem has been described, ask the class to think of themselves as movie directors. Their first assignment is to think about the issue and figure out how many players are needed to act it out. List all the parts on the board. It is usually effective for the person with the problem to play the person with whom they are having the problem. This gives the student a chance to experience another point of view. But there are many exceptions to this guideline. The people involved in the problem may benefit most by watching the role-play. Boys can play girls' parts, and visa versa.

Based on the problem description, review the spoken lines and actions of each player, and ask for volunteers to play out the scene. Have them act out the scene in the middle of the circle, and remind them not to worry whether it's right or not. If, after playing it out once, any changes are needed to make it more accurate, they can try again. Kids love to role-play and sometimes beg to replay the scene over and over. They especially like playing the part of the teacher and watching the teacher pretend to be one of the students.

After the role-play, ask the players what they were thinking, feeling, or deciding according to the parts they were playing. It's very important to have the students express their responses after each role-play, so they can learn the results of what is happening. For example, a punishment may stop the behavior and seem to solve the problem. But the student may decide, "I'm a bad person," or, "I'll get even later." Processing responses can help students find solutions to problems that will lead to healthy, long-term results.

One girl was upset with a boy who threw food at her in the cafeteria, and she put this on the agenda. The kids loved role-playing this scene. When asked what they were thinking, feeling, or deciding, the kids who were role-playing other kids in the cafeteria said it was fun and scary. Some were afraid they might get in trouble, and they wished some adult would do something. The boy playing the food thrower said it was fun and that he felt good because everyone noticed him. The girl playing the target of the food throwing felt upset and embarrassed and didn't want to go back to the cafeteria again. Understanding feelings and decisions helped the kids when they brainstormed for solutions.

## *Brainstorming*

Teach your students about brainstorming—a process in which they think of as many ideas as possible in a short period of time. When brainstorming, it's fun to think of silly or outrageous ideas to start creative juices flowing. Silly ideas often lead to practical ideas. Every opinion is important, so write every idea on the board. During the brainstorming time, don't analyze or criticize any suggestion. Writing a brainstorm suggestion down doesn't mean it could really work; it's just a suggestion. Explain that there will be time later to eliminate suggestions that might be impractical or disrespectful.

Recording every suggestion tells all students that every opinion is important and worthy of consideration. When students know they can present an idea without its being judged, it frees them to take more chances to contribute instead of playing it safe for fear of looking foolish. Once the list of suggestions is completed, discuss them and let the students conclude what ideas would or would not be effective solutions. Then let them decide what ideas can be crossed off the list because of disrespectfulness or impracticality.

For students who use brainstorming time to be silly, writing down their ideas often influences them to stop shouting out things they don't really mean. One day during a brainstorming session, one of the students suggested, "Just yell at them." The teacher ignored the suggestion. The student started repeating her suggestion in a louder and louder voice until the class meeting was disrupted. If the teacher had written down the suggestion right away, the student might have stopped.

Brainstorming can be used with or without role playing; however, role playing should usually be followed by brainstorming. After the role-play, tell the kids it's time to brainstorm. Explain that anyone can give a suggestion of what would make the situation better. Remind them that there are no right or wrong answers during brainstorming. Sometimes ideas that seem impractical or even impossible give rise to good solutions. Sometimes silly suggestions help people lighten up and start being creative. Here is the list the students generated by brainstorming after role-playing the food-throwing problem:

1. The boy who threw food could apologize.
2. The girl could throw food back.
3. A teacher could tell them to stop.
4. The boy could be sent to the office.
5. The girl could move to another seat.
6. She could tell the cafeteria monitor.
7. She could say, "Stop throwing food at me."
8. She could ignore it.
9. She could wear a catcher's mitt.

The student who put the problem on the agenda was asked to choose the one she liked best from the list of ideas. She chose number 4, sending the boy to the office. The teacher asked her how that would help her. "Would it make you feel good if he gets in trouble?"

The girl thought about that and then asked if she could change her mind. She chose number 1, having the boy apologize. The teacher asked the boy if he would be willing to apologize. He said yes. The teacher asked if he would like to apologize now at the class meeting or later in private. He agreed to apologize now, which he did. This example illustrates three important class-meeting techniques:

1. Allow the student who put the problem on the agenda to choose the suggestion that will be most helpful.

2. Ask, "How will that help?"
3. Allow the student to choose between two times for following through on the chosen suggestion.

When students are allowed to choose the suggestion they think will be most helpful, they are increasing their accountability and responsibility. Students are encouraged to think of long-range results when asked, "How will that help you, the class, or another person?" Choosing when they want to follow through on the suggestion increases their sense of power in a useful direction. Whichever solution is chosen, it should be tried for at least one week. If it doesn't work, anyone can put the issue back on the agenda.

## *Voting*

If the students involved in the problem can't agree on a solution or want the class to offer guidance, ask for a show of hands to find out how many think each of the brainstormed solutions will help solve the problem. They can discuss why or why not. Use the show of hands as a vote, and let the class choose a solution. In this case, the majority rules. As long as the solution is just for a week and students have an opportunity to reevaluate or put the item back on the agenda, voting often gets things accomplished more quickly.

Voting is appropriate when the problem being discussed involves the whole class, such as which kind of party they would like to choose from the brainstorming list, or which plan they like best for handling recess problems. In some cases, a majority vote is appropriate, but there are some cases in which it is imperative for the class to reach consensus.

A consensus is needed if deciding on a solution would leave a disgruntled minority who uses their power to defeat or get revenge on the rest of the class. Since one of the goals of class meetings is to teach students to find solutions that everyone can live with, it is better to wait for consensus than to expect students to agree to a solution that won't work for them. Most problems presented for solving are not the kind that pit one part of the class against another. Unless it's really worth the time and effort, use a majority vote whenever possible.

### Appreciations

A helpful and positive conclusion to the problem-solving process is encouraging students to express appreciations. After the class has role-played, brainstormed, and chosen a suggestion to try for one week, ask the students if anyone has an appreciation for the person who put the problem on the agenda, for the role players, or for the person who made the mistake. Encourage kids to be honest and to speak directly to the person, using positive statements to let them know their contribution is appreciated.

For example, in a class where the item on the agenda was about a boy who insulted another student, one girl who had experienced similar insults said during the appreciations session, "I want to thank you for bringing this up. A lot of kids make fun of me, and I never knew what to do. Now I have an idea of how to handle it next time it happens to me." Another student said, "I want to thank you for bringing this up because it was so much fun to role-play. I like to tease people, and the role-play gave me an acceptable way to do it."

As students practice new skills, it's best to start problem solving with situations at school, although it's also possible to solve certain home problems with these classroom methods. When dealing with problems outside the classroom, brainstorm suggestions that will help the student decide what to do. Use your judgment about the maturity of the kids and your own comfort level for handling such problems.

## The Power of Class Meetings in Difficult Situations

When kids get really skilled at problem solving, they can be extremely encouraging. In one school, the class had a problem with a student who came to school smelling badly of urine. He was a bed wetter. The kids teased him mercilessly on the playground. Someone put the problem on the agenda, and the students gave suggestions that would be helpful rather than hurtful. They learned that the boy didn't have a washing machine or even a shower at home. One of the students offered to have him come by his house every morning to shower and put on clean clothes, which he could wash the night before in their washer.

In one school where every teacher was using class meetings, the special-education teacher described in a faculty meeting how badly she felt when the other kids called her students such names as "retards." All the teachers agreed to discuss this problem in their class meetings. They asked the students several questions, such as how they felt when people teased them and called them names. They asked if they had ever thought about how much it must hurt the special-education students when they called them names. Most kids really don't think about the long-range results of their behavior unless they are invited to do so. They were asked, "How many of you feel good about being mean to others?" None of them admitted this possibility. The students in each class were then asked for suggestions to solve the problem of hurting other people through name calling. They came up with solutions that went beyond eliminating the name calling, deciding on ways to help the special-education students feel included in their games and activities.

In still another school, a little girl was killed in a car accident. The crisis team decided to use class meetings to help the kids deal with their grief and their fears. In each class they replaced compliments with a celebration of how this little girl had touched them. Each student had a chance to express an appreciation for the girl who had died. Then the teachers asked their students, "What are your concerns now?" Some of them were afraid to go home. Many had never dealt with death before and didn't know what to do. They brainstormed and found several suggestions. One was to set up a phone tree so they could call each other, even in the middle of the night. They came up with a list of people they could talk to during the day. Many kids had different people they felt they could talk to during school hours: janitors, librarians, a lunchroom supervisor, counselors, teachers, the principal, and each other. It was decided that students could get passes to go talk to someone whenever they felt the need. They decided to make pictures of the girl on a ribbon pin, which they wore for a week in her memory. They planted a tree, which they purchased and nurtured throughout the year in memory of the girl. The kids became role models for adult school members on the many ways to deal with grief.

Bronia Grunwald, coauthor with Rudolf Dreikurs and Floy Pepper of *Maintaining Sanity in the Classroom,* is a teacher who used class meetings for over twenty-five years. Bronia had such faith in the class-meeting process that she asked for all the problem kids. Her philosophy was: The more problems, the more opportunity to teach problem-solving skills. She also had classrooms with over forty students. During an interview she said, "That many students made more work correcting papers and having conferences with parents, but I also had more students to help solve the problems." Even though Bronia had mostly "problem" students, by mid-year their behavior problems were eliminated because they had learned mutual respect, cooperation, and problem-solving skills.

But Bronia did not simply coast through the rest of the year. When she'd notice that a colleague was having trouble with a student, during a class meeting she would ask her students, "How would you feel about inviting Janey from Mrs. Smith's class join our class? She is having problems. How many of you think we could help her?" Every time, her class would enthusiastically agree to invite a problem student into their class so they could use their skills to help.

We hope you're developing an understanding of how class meetings can empower students. Where else do they have their thoughts and ideas taken seriously? Where else do they have an opportunity to learn life skills that build confidence, courage, and self-esteem? Where else do they have an opportunity to nurture each other and learn respectful interactions? How could these benefits *not* create a classroom environment that enhances academic learning as well as emotional growth? Everything improves in a nurturing climate. Students and teachers can flourish.

# Why People Do What They Do

**A**fter forming a circle, exchanging compliments, and choosing an agenda item, explain to the students that at this class meeting they will be learning about the beliefs behind behavior. We are much more effective when we understand the belief that motivates a person's behavior instead of just dealing with the behavior itself. Use this candle activity to demonstrate the power of the belief behind behavior.

### Materials

1. Four candles of varying sizes to represent a mother, a father, a four-year-old girl and a baby.
2. Four small candle holders.
3. Kitchen matches.
4. The *Family Songs* audiotape.[1]
5. A cassette tape player.

[1]Wayne Frieden and Marie Hartwell-Walker, *Family Songs* audiotape, from Sunrise Books, Tapes, and Videos, 1-800-456-7770.

1. Deliver the following short lecture. "There is a belief behind every behavior, but what do we usually deal with? The behavior. That makes as much sense as ignoring an arsonist who keeps setting fires. Dealing with the arsonist does not mean you don't also put out the fire. Dealing with the belief behind the behavior does not mean you don't deal with the behavior. You are most effective when you are aware of both possibilities, the behavior itself *and* the belief behind the behavior.

"Here's the classic example of a belief behind a behavior. Suppose you have a four-year-old daughter. You go off to the hospital and bring home a brand new baby. What does the four-year-old see happening? Mom gives the baby lots of time and attention. What does the four-year-old interpret that to mean? Mom loves the baby more than me. What does the four-year-old do in an attempt to get the love back? She acts like a baby—whines, cries, wants a bottle, soils her pants."

2. Play a few lines of the song "Number One" on the *Family Songs* tape. Introduce it by saying, "I'd like to play a song for you that beautifully illustrates this point."

> Oh, it's hard to be number one
> And lately it's just no fun at all.
> Life was so nice when we were three—
> Mommy and Daddy and me.
>
> When I was the only one,
> Everyone noticed me.
> They said what a cute little baby—
> What a handsome child he'll be.
> And now there's another,
> And I don't like it one bit.
> Send it back to the hospital and
> Let's just forget about it.

3. Use candles for the following demonstration. "Now I would like to demonstrate what one mother did because she had a four-year-old daughter who was feeling displaced by the birth of a baby brother. One evening, when the baby was asleep, the mother sat down at the kitchen table with her daughter and said, 'Honey, I'd like to tell you a story about our family. These candles represent our family.' She picked up one long candle and said, 'This is the mommy candle. This one is for me.' She took a match and lit the candle as she said, 'This flame represents my love.' She picked up another long candle and said, 'This candle is the daddy candle.' She used the flame from the mommy candle to light the daddy candle and said, 'When I married your daddy, I gave him all my love—and I still have all my love left.' She put the daddy candle in a candle holder, picked up a smaller candle, and said, 'This candle is for you.' She lit a smaller candle with the flame from her candle and said, 'When you were born, I gave you all my love. And look. Daddy still has all my love, and I still have all my love left.' The mother put that candle in a candle holder next to the daddy candle, then picked up the smallest candle and, while lighting it with the mommy candle, said 'This is a candle for your baby brother. When he was born, I gave him all my love. And look—you still have all my love. Daddy has all my love. And I still have all my love left because that is the way love is. You can give it all to everyone you love and still have all your love. Now look at all the light we have in our family with all this love.'"

4. Allow silence, for the students to experience their feelings. Allow time for expressing feelings and thoughts. In addition to using the candle activity, leading a discussion is an excellent method of

helping kids understand why people do what they do. Sometimes questions that require a simple "yes" or "no" answer are enough to get the class engaged and wanting to know more. At other times it is important to ask open-ended questions, the kind that inspire more than "yes," "no," and "I don't know" answers.

### ▼ Building Block 7: Recognizing the Four Reasons People Do What They Do

Ask your students if they've ever wondered why people do what they do, and if they would like to learn more. Usually they do, and they'll raise their hands to tell you their ideas. After hearing what they have to say, tell them, "In addition, there are Four Mistaken Goals of Misbehavior. To explain these four mistaken goals, I'd like to use the example of homework. What reasons do you think kids might have for not doing their homework?"

The kids will usually give such reasons as "I was too tired," "I had too much other work," "I lost it," "I didn't understand it," and so on. Explain that these are the rational excuses people give for their behavior. However, many times people do things for reasons that are not rational, and they may not even be aware of the reasons. We call these hidden reasons. The hidden reasons for behavior are based on our desire to belong and feel important. Ask, "How many of you want to feel like you belong and are important in your family, with your friends, in the classroom?"

All of us seek ways of belonging and being important. Sometimes they work, and sometimes they don't. If we think we aren't loved or don't belong, we usually try something to get the love back, or else we hurt others to get

68

even when we think they don't love us. Sometimes we even feel like giving up because we think it's impossible to do things right and to belong. The things we do when we believe we don't belong and aren't important are often mistaken ways of finding belonging and importance. The Four Mistaken Goals of Misbehavior are below.

1. Undue Attention
2. Power
3. Revenge
4. Assumed Disability (Giving Up)

Go back to the example of homework. Ask, "How many of you think some people might not do their homework because that's a good way to get the teacher or their parents to pay more attention to them? Have any of you ever decided not to do your homework to show your power and prove that teachers or parents can't make you—or at least they can't make you do it as fast as they want or as thoroughly as they want?" (Watch closely for nonverbal signals such as a grin, a flustered face, etc. which we call a recognition reflex.) "Maybe some of you have felt hurt and decided to get even by not doing your homework because you knew that would hurt your parents or teacher. Have any of you ever felt so discouraged that you believed you couldn't do your homework, so why try? Did you ever want to just give up and have people leave you alone?"

## The Mistaken Goal Chart[2]

Ask your students to think of a time they felt unloved, thought they weren't special, or felt they didn't belong. Tell them to try to remember exactly what happened, how they

[2]See Appendix C for a more detailed version of a Mistaken Goal Chart.

| Mistaken Goal Chart | | | |
|---|---|---|---|
| **Thinking/ Deciding** | **Feeling** | **Behavior** | **Mistaken Goal** |
| | Irritated<br>Worried<br>Annoyed | | |
| | Angry<br>Mad<br>Frustrated | | |
| | Hurt<br>Upset<br>Sad<br>Disappointed | | |
| | Hopeless<br>Helpless | | |

felt, and what they decided to do. Give them about two minutes to relive the situation in their minds. Then, put up a chart on the board, with four columns, like the one shown below. In the second column, list four groups of words that express feelings.

Ask your students to look at the chart, and see if any of the feeling words apply to the situation they were thinking about. If they weren't able to think of a situation, all they need do is think of a time they had any of the feelings on the list. Ask for a volunteer to share his or her example. Find an example for each of the groups of feeling words. In the third column, write down what the volunteers did when they had those feelings. In the first column, write what the volunteers were thinking or deciding when they had those feelings. Below is a chart filled out by volunteers in a third-grade class.

| Mistaken Goal Chart | | | |
|---|---|---|---|
| Thinking/ Deciding | Feeling | Behavior | Mistaken Goal |
| Teacher only pays attention to the smart kids. | Irritated Worried Annoyed | I make funny noises and make fun of her when she's not looking. | Undue attention (to keep others busy with him) |
| The playground supervisor tells me I have to eat my lunch, or I can't play. | Angry Mad Frustrated | I pretend to eat my sand- wich, but I hide it in my pocket | Power (to be boss) |
| Someone called me "Fatso." | Hurt Upset Sad Disappointed | I said, "You're ugly." I cried so no one could hear me. | Revenge (to get even) |
| I'll never be able to do my times tables! | Hopeless Helpless | I said, "I hate math and I think it's stupid." I threw my paper in the trash. | Give up and be left alone |

After filling in the chart, explain to your students that everyone gets discouraged at times. When discouraged, we have those feelings, think those thoughts, or act those ways. In the chart, behavior is listed as one of the Four Mistaken Goals of Misbehavior. Write them in the fourth column: Undue Attention, Power, Revenge, and Assumed Disability (Giving Up).

71

It is important to understand the different beliefs behind behavior, in order to avoid using the same solution. Once we understand the reasons why people do what they do, we might be able to think of ways to encourage them when they are feeling discouraged. With the class, use brainstorming skills and make lists of encouragement.

**Activity:** Have the students go back over each of the mistaken goals and think of things that would encourage a person who had those discouraging thoughts. Ask the kids what would make them feel better if, as in Undue Attention, they believed they are valued only if they are noticed or getting special service. For Power, what if they believed they had to be the boss, do it their way, win, or show others they can't force them to do something? For Revenge, what would be encouraging for students who believe it's okay to hurt others or themselves because *they* feel hurt. For Assumed Disability, what would motivate those who believe it's better not to try, who wish everyone would leave them alone because they are sure they aren't good enough or can't do things right.

As the class brainstorms encouragement ideas, write them down on a chart, like the one shown on the next page, for future class meetings. To help the kids with ideas, ask, "How could a person get attention or special treatment without misbehaving? How could a person have power without having power over other people? How can people handle hurt feelings without hurting themselves and others? How can people get help learning a skill or learn that it's okay to make mistakes?"

Following on page 74 is an Encouragement Chart filled out by a fifth grade class.

After the class has completed this activity, you might want to present some practice situations so they can guess the mistaken goal and suggest appropriate encouragement. Remind the students all we really can do is guess,

| Encouragement Chart | | | |
|---|---|---|---|
| **Undue Attention** | **Power** | **Revenge** | **Assumed Disability** |
| | | | |

and that it isn't up to us to tell others why they do what they do. If we guess correctly, we may help others become aware of their hidden reasons, which is often helpful. Even if we're wrong, that gives us information to build on.

When guessing is done with a friendly, helpful attitude, the people we are guessing about usually let us know if we're right because they feel understood. Sometimes they let us know by a smile of recognition, and sometimes with a simple "yes" or "no." The important point is that they know we're trying to help, not to hurt or stereotype.

Use the following examples to let students practice their new knowledge. (Explain that these are imaginary names and situations.)

Example 1. Jesse refuses to turn in a homework assignment even though it is completed.

Example 2. Emily leaves her seat twenty times a day.

Example 3. Serita carves on her desk.

Example 4. Charlie always walks in two minutes late and the whole class has to stop what they're doing to wait for him to sit down.

Example 5. Luke calls someone names on the school bus.

Here is an Encouragement Chart filled out by a fifth grade class.

| Encouragement Chart | | | |
|---|---|---|---|
| **Undue Attention** | **Power** | **Revenge** | **Assumed Disability** |
| Walk with them to school. | Ask for their ideas. | Tell them you are sorry if you hurt their feelings. | Let them help someone else with something they are good at. |
| Sit by them at lunch. | Let them be a line leader. | Be their friend. | Tell them they are okay. |
| Laugh at their stories. | Put them in charge of a project or chore. | Invite them to your birthday party. | Have another student work with them. |
| Talk to them. | Ask for their help to tutor another student. | Compliment them. | Tell them math was hard for you, too. |
| Let them have a special job. | Ask them to teach the class how to play a game. | Ask them to play a game with you. | Let them do the things they are good at. |
| Ask them to play. | Tell them you feel angry when they boss everyone around. | Give them a hug. | Tell them they will get it when they are ready. |

While any of the above behaviors could be based on more than one belief, damaging property or hurting another person is usually a form of revenge. When we have a real situation on the agenda and make guesses about the belief, one way we know we've guessed correctly is if the person misbehaving lets us know. Another way is to watch the person's body language and look for a recognition reflex. Remember, that people are often unaware of the belief behind their own behavior. But when their motivation is guessed in a friendly way, they usually see the truth themselves and feel understood. (They can also tell when people are trying to guess in order to have information to use against them.)

You may want to go back to the person who put the food-throwing issue on the agenda (in Chapter 5) and ask if she or the class knows why the other person might have thrown food. Use the Mistaken Goal Chart as a reference.

**Activity:** One class decided to make signs on the ends of Popsicle sticks for each of the mistaken goals. Each student had a set of four. They agreed that if anyone was behaving in a disruptive way, they would guess what the mistaken belief might be and hold up their sign. The intent would not be to label, blame, or stereotype, but it could be seen by the other person as a friendly reminder. The misbehaving student could then decide if he or she would like to choose contributing behavior instead of disruptive behavior.

There is an amusing footnote to this story. Guess who got the Power sign the most often? The teacher. This good-natured teacher would say, "Okay, okay. I can see that I'm trying to boss you around. Who has some ideas about what I could do to invite cooperation?" This teacher modeled that it is not "bad" to make a mistake, and that the group can help each other make effective changes.

**Activity:** Play the *Behavior Songs*[3] for each of the four mistaken goals. After each song, ask (with a sense of fun) if any of the behaviors mentioned in this song sound familiar. You can also watch for recognition reflexes (laughter, grins, head nodding) while the songs are being played. Lead a discussion on what the kids think about the mistaken belief in each song, and their suggestions about how the kids in the songs could be encouraged.

Even though these activities are time-consuming, you are laying the groundwork for respectful and effective problem solving. Don't be too surprised if student behavior starts improving spontaneously. We are all often unaware of why we do what we do. That's why it can be helpful just to hold up a mirror. Students will also have more understanding and compassion for other students, and the atmosphere in the classroom will improve.

[3]Wayne Frieden and Marie Hartwell-Walker, *Behavior Songs* audiotape, from Sunrise Books, Tapes, and Videos, 1-800-456-7770.

# Logical Consequences and Other Nonpunitive Solutions

**T**eachers are often disrespectful of and discouraging to young people, without even realizing it. Any form of punishment *or* permissiveness is both disrespectful and discouraging. Common forms of punishment found in our schools include the following: sending students to the principal, having them pick up garbage on the grounds, calling home to tell parents their children are in trouble at school, putting a child's name on the board, humiliating students in front of their classmates, plus detention and suspension.

Most teachers mean well when they administer punishment. They believe punishment is the best way to motivate students to behave properly. If the misbehavior stops for a while because of punishment, they may have been fooled into thinking they were right. However, when they become aware of the long-range effects of punishment on students, they naturally want to learn more respectful methods of motivating students to behave properly. While students who are punished may comply, their behavior is motivated by the fear of getting into trouble instead of the desire of learning self-discipline. Other students openly or passively rebel in response to punishment.

Although kids hate being punished themselves, they can be very reluctant to give up the power to punish others. It takes time for them to learn to use power in positive ways instead of trying to have power *over* others. There are several alternatives a teacher can use, or teach students to use, if the problem solving becomes disruptive, disrespectful, or difficult in some way.

When you first begin to hold class meetings, you may notice that students tend to think up very punitive suggestions while brainstorming. Many of their ideas are modeled on their experiences with punitive parents and teachers. Children live what they learn.

Teachers must take the first step to eliminate humiliation and punishment in order to create an environment that is nurturing, respectful, and more conducive for learning. Teachers can help young people follow their lead by teaching skills for finding solutions that are nonpunitive. You will need an entire class meeting (after compliments and follow-up on prior solutions) to teach the eighth and final building block for successful class meetings. Explain that today's meeting will be dedicated to learning another important form of encouragement, finding nonpunitive solutions to problems. The focus will be on using consequences instead of punishment.

## ▼ Building Block 8: Applying Logical Consequences and Other Nonpunitive Solutions

**Activity:** Ask the following questions, and write students' answers on the board: "What is the first thing you want to do when someone hurts you? What do you want to do when someone bosses you? What do you want to do when someone calls you names or puts you down? How many of you think any of these things help you *behave* better?" Ask for a volunteer to make the following poster to help them remember that encouragement is more effective than punishment.

---

**Where did we ever get the crazy idea that to make people *do* better, first we have to make them *feel* worse? People *do* better when they *feel* better.**

---

**Activity:** Ask the students to think of a time when someone tried to motivate them to do better by making them feel worse. Ask them to try to remember exactly what happened as though they were reliving the event, and also to recall how they felt. As a result of that experience, what did they decide about themselves, about others, or about what to do? Invite sharing, one student at a time. Make a chart, like the one below, and list the answers, as well as all the things that were done by way of punishment.

| My Punishment | What I Decided About Myself and/or Others | What I Decided to Do |
|---|---|---|
| Stay after class. | The teacher is stupid. | Stay after, pretend to work. |
| Call my parents. | I'm in trouble. I need to figure out how to get out of it. | Tell my parents the teacher lied. |
| Write sentences. | This is boring and stupid. I'd better not get caught again. | Write the sentences and then do what I want. |
| Name on board. | I don't care. | Experience the punishment, but don't change. |

Make sure the list includes grounding, spanking, scolding, and taking away privileges.

Point out that although many teachers use punishment because they think it will help students learn, that still doesn't make it effective. Ask the students, "How many of you think that the kids in the above example are deciding to be more responsible and cooperative in the future? What other things do you think they might be deciding to do in the future?"

Teachers often do things for the same reasons kids do, because they don't know another way. Find out how many students are willing to learn some alternatives to help them learn from mistakes and encourage improved behavior. The following activity increases understanding of the difference between consequences and punishment.

# The Three Rs of Logical Consequences

**Activity:** Have the kids work on a problem about two imaginary students who were late from recess twice. On the board, list five suggestions for solving that problem, including the following: (1) the boys have to miss recess for a week; (2) the boys have to stay after school and make up the time they missed; (3) the boys have to play closer to the bell so they can hear it; (4) the class will assign a buddy to remind the boys to come in on time; and (5) let them come in whenever they want to, but it's their job to catch up on what they missed.

Now tell the students about the Three Rs of Logical Consequences: related, respectful, and reasonable. *Related* means the consequence is directly related to the behavior. For example, when students don't do their homework, sending them to the office is not related to missed homework. A related consequence would be to have them make up the homework or not get points for that assignment. *Respectful* means enforcing the consequence with dignity and respect: "Would you like to make up the homework assignment during lunch recess, or right after school?" *Reasonable* means you don't add punishment such as, "Now you'll have to do twice as much."

Go over the list of the five suggestions on the board. For each suggestion, ask, by a show of hands, "How many think this suggestion is related, respectful, and reasonable?" Cross out the suggestions that do not fit the criteria of the Three Rs of Logical Consequences. Point out that when a consequence meets all three Rs, it will probably be a good alternative to punishment.

There is one more important component of consequences that are nonpunitive. Students should have knowledge of the rules in advance. We call this "revealed."

*Revealed* means the students know in advance that if they don't do their homework, they'll need to make it up or else risk getting a poor grade.

To make this point with your students, ask, "How many of you would feel it would be respectful if you had to experience a consequence for something you did not know about? For instance, suppose the teacher decided that anyone who sat in a certain chair would be suspended, but she didn't tell anyone?"

## Going Beyond Consequences

Logical consequences can be misused. Sometimes teachers and students may think they are disguising punishment by using the words *logical consequences*. Here are seven suggestions for ensuring that consequences are not disguised punishment.

1. *If it isn't obvious, it isn't logical.* One of the most popular questions we hear is, "What would be the logical consequence for _____ ?" The answer is, "If a consequence is not obvious, then a consequence probably is not logical or appropriate." For example, it is obvious that if a child draws on a wall or a desk, it would be related, respectful, and reasonable for that child to clean the wall or desk (or, if very young, at least *help* clean the wall or desk). If we have to struggle to identify a logical consequence, it's a clue that we might be headed for a punishment instead of a solution.

2. *Focus on solutions instead of consequences.* Make sure solutions are helpful, not hurtful. The poster (see Figure 4.2) "We are here to help each other," is a good reminder. Some people get fixated on conse-

quences and forget the ultimate goal of helping. The most effective strategy is to look for solutions. It is a mistake to think there must be a logical consequence for every behavior or to solve every problem. Put less emphasis on consequences and more emphasis on solving the problem.

3. *Involve the kids in solutions.* Young people are our greatest untapped resource. They have a wealth of wisdom and talent for solving problems, and numerous benefits result when they become involved. When kids participate in finding solutions, not only do they use and strengthen their skills, they are also more likely to keep agreements because they have ownership. They develop self-confidence and self-esteem when they are listened to, taken seriously, and valued for their contributions. Because they feel part of the classroom community, they have less motivation to misbehave and are more willing to work on solutions to problems.

4. *Focus on the future instead of the past.* Rather than focusing on making students "pay" for what they've done, look for solutions that will help them learn for the future. One fifth grade class was trying to help a student unhappy about another student who scribbled on his spelling test while correcting it. One suggestion was that the scribbler spend half an hour in study hall; another was to give the scribbler an extra piece of paper to scribble on while correcting tests. The first suggestion focuses on making the scribbler pay for the mistake, while the second focuses on helping him solve the problem in the future.

5. *Make the opportunity-responsibility-consequence connection.* Every opportunity has a related responsibility. The obvious consequence for not wanting the responsibility is to lose the opportunity. For instance,

kids have the opportunity to use the playground during recess. The related responsibility is to treat the equipment and other people with respect. When people or things are treated disrespectfully, the logical consequence is losing the opportunity of using the playground and sitting on a bench. To instill a sense of responsibility, accountability, and empowerment, say to your student, "You decide how much time you think you need to cool off and calm down. Let me know when you are ready to use the playground respectfully." Consequences are effective only if they are enforced respectfully and students are given another opportunity as soon as they are ready for the responsibility.

6. *Avoid piggybacking.* Piggybacking is adding something to the consequences that isn't necessary and is actually hurtful, such as, "Maybe this will teach you!" or, "You can just sit there and think about what you did!" It's easy to make the mistake of turning consequences into punishment by piggybacking because it's based on the belief that in order to make people do better, first we have to make them feel worse.

Adults often use piggybacking to add punishment to something that would otherwise be a natural or logical consequence, or a solution that would work without punishment. In one class, two students agreed to a suggestion to solve their problem of being late after recess. Instead of letting them try out their solution, the teacher wanted to solve a problem that hadn't even occurred yet. She asked the class to discuss what the consequence would be if the boys were late again. The class seemed to pick up her piggybacking mentality. They came up with several suggestions, but instead of being helpful, most of their solutions sounded punitive. They voted on sending the two boys to the principal.

Later that day, the teacher came across the two boys, who were in tears because they thought being sent to the principal was unfair. They felt ganged up on, and that they were treated disrespectfully. They were right. She told the boys that she had made a mistake, explaining what it was. Then she asked if they would be willing to let her try again at the next class meeting so she could correct her mistake. The boys stopped crying and said, "Okay, but do we have to go to the principal?" "No," she said. "Just stick with your choice to play closer to the bell. If that doesn't work, we can try again at the class meeting to come up with another plan, but one that isn't hurtful. Okay?"

7. *Plan consequences in advance.* One way to avoid the feeling of punishment is to get students involved in deciding on consequences in advance. During a class meeting or a problem-solving session, ask the students for help in determining what consequences would help them learn. For example, "What do you think would be logical to help classmates remember to use the school equipment respectfully?" "What do you think a logical consequence would be when you return books to the library late?" If students aren't involved in the planning, at least give them advance notice. For instance, inform them that people who abuse the special resource display area may be asked to leave the area until they are ready to use the area respectfully again. Often, teachers get so excited about consequences that they think they are the only alternative to punishment. In fact, there are many other alternatives, including those discussed below.

## Encourage Emotional Honesty

Explain to your students how to use this formula for emotional honesty: "I feel _____ about _____ because _____ ." For instance, "I feel uncomfort-able about this consequence because I think it is hurtful [or unrelated, or disrespectful, or unreasonable]." Tell them that it's your job to help them use their many skills to help each other, not hurt each other. "Since this consequence is hurtful, I haven't done my job yet. We'll try again tomorrow."

## Use Questions That Redirect Thinking

Another approach is asking students whether they think the consequence would motivate any of them to be more cooperative and/or feel a sense of belonging in the class. This question invites them to be more realistic about what is helpful and to focus on positive solutions that work instead of negative solutions that hurt.

During the learning process, you can help students improve their skills by asking them, "How is this suggested consequence related, respectful, and reasonable?" Some teachers wait until all the brainstorming ideas are listed and then ask, "Which ones should be eliminated because they are not related, not respectful, or not reasonable?"

## Trust the Process

Another alternative is simply trusting the process and letting the students make mistakes. If a consequence is not hurtful or humiliating, a teacher might let it go and allow the students to discover why something that isn't related and reasonable doesn't work. At the next class meeting, you can always put the new problem created by the mistake on the agenda. It is important to work on progress, not perfection.

### Teach Accountability

There is a big difference between punishment and holding kids accountable with dignity and respect. Often, students don't like being held accountable, thinking it's the same thing as being punished. But it's crucial to instill a sense of accountability in kids—even if they don't like it at first. When punishment is eliminated and consequences are both kind and firm, kids usually gain self-worth that results from being respectful to themselves and others. When students experience these alternatives to punishment, they gain courage, confidence, and life-skills that will help them live successfully in our society.

▼
## CHAPTER
# 8

# Putting It All Together

In your preparatory class meetings, you have introduced, demonstrated, and practiced the Eight Building Blocks listed in Chapter 3. Let's review them here.

### Eight Building Blocks for Effective Class Meetings: A Review

1. Forming a circle.
2. Practicing compliments and appreciations.
3. Creating an agenda.
4. Developing communication skills.
5. Learning about separate realities.
6. Solving problems through role playing and brainstorming.
7. Recognizing the four reasons people do what they do.

8. Applying logical consequences and other non-punitive solutions.

If you or your students don't understand any of the eight building blocks, now is the time to review. Once you have the basics down, you can begin holding regular meetings that follow the class meeting format reviewed below.

### Class Meeting Format

1. Compliments and appreciations.
2. Follow-up on prior solutions.
3. Agenda items.
   a. Share feelings while others listen.
   b. Discuss without fixing.
   c. Ask for problem-solving help.
4. Future plans (field trips, parties, projects).

### Follow-up on Prior Solutions

Check the status of what the students learned at previous meetings. Follow up on the solutions chosen during problem-solving sessions. Remember that any suggested solution is to be tried only for a week, so it's important to ask if the solution has been working. If it hasn't, you may wish to put the issue back on the agenda for future problem solving.

### Agenda Items

When an agenda item is read, ask the student with the issue if he or she still wants help with it. If so, ask what a satisfactory solution could be. Ask the offending party if he or she agrees. If not, ask the offending party what his or her idea of a solution would be. If both students agree, ask if they would try out the solution for one week, and then move on to the next agenda item. Not all problems require role playing, brainstorming, or even class discussion. But if the parties don't agree on a solution, have the rest of the class brainstorm for suggestions.

Many teachers go around the circle twice when brainstorming so everyone has a second chance to either make a comment or to pass. This draws out the quieter students and gives the less courageous kids time to think and listen for ideas from their classmates.

Sometimes, as you go around the circle, there will be students who don't comment and don't pass. Rather than passing them by and assuming they have nothing to say, ask, "Are you thinking or are you passing?" If they say they are thinking, ask, "Would you like us to wait while you think, or would you like us to come back to you?" When you present limited choices, students learn how to contribute usefully and can save face if the delay was merely a way of being silly or rebellious.

When the brainstorming is finished, allow the student who put the item on the agenda to choose the suggestion he or she thinks would be the most helpful. Ask the student to try the solution for one week.

Remind the class that there don't have to be consequences for everything. Often, simply discussing the problem and hearing how others feel about it can motivate a student to change. If a discussion doesn't solve things and the problem occurs again, it can always be put back on the agenda.

Another option for handling agenda items is to give students the choice simply to express their feelings. It's important to let kids know that it's okay to share their feelings—feelings are always okay and that they are different from actions. When a student is expressing feelings, it's important just to listen without trying to fix the problem. It's up to the person who put the item on the agenda to specify which approach he or she prefers.

If a student wants to talk about a problem that involves someone else—such as a bus driver, another teacher, a student who is absent, or the principal—remind him that the class can't talk about anyone unless he or she is present. If the person isn't willing to come to the room, the problem can be discussed only in terms of what the student can do.

Effective problem solving empowers students and encourages them to have confidence in their ability to help one another. It emphasizes that learning is a continuing process that includes mistakes and stresses the importance of respect for self and others. Dealing with the student's real concerns is a great advantage because it teaches them that they can come up with enough good ideas to help each other. They don't need to pass the buck by sending classmates to the principal for punishment.

## Future Plans

Take time during class meetings to plan a fun classroom activity, a field trip, a party, or a special treat. This time can be used creatively. A third-grade class discussed what to do when they got fidgety. The teacher had a tape player in his room. He agreed with his students that when they got fidgety, he'd turn on loud rock music and let them dance wildly for two minutes. When the music went off, everyone sat back down. A sixth grade class planned for a special game-board tournament on Friday afternoons for students who had completed their assignments. Once you have established regular class meetings, students will begin to feel closer to you and to each other. Setting up a party or time to play is a treat that everyone enjoys.

## Remembering That the Process Takes Time

When kids are learning a new way of looking at things and new ways of handling problems, sometimes things get worse before they get better. If the kids aren't responding with the enthusiasm you'd hoped for, don't be discouraged. Keep plugging away, in small steps, and trust that they will all come together eventually to help the class.

If you find your students struggling because of their lack of skills, use the class meetings to continue building skills before tackling items on the agenda. Remind yourself and your students that it's okay to take time for training. Even if the class meetings are difficult at first, don't give up. They will get better with practice. If you practice taking small steps, you'll see steady improvement.

Some kids respond immediately; others take longer. We met with two teacher two months after a teacher in-service. They said, "We are so thankful that you warned us that it sometimes takes a month or more before things run smoothly. Our first class meetings were so discouraging that, without warning, we would have given up. We're glad we stuck it out because it has made such a difference in our classrooms."

In the next chapter, we cover many skills that can enhance class meetings. Many of these skills can also be used during regular class time.

# CHAPTER
# 9

# Expanding
# Class-Meeting Skills

**O**nce you have become familiar with the basics of holding class meetings, you'll soon notice how helpful it would be to have additional skills for dealing with difficult situations. As your skills increase, you can help your students improve their ability to cooperate and succeed in class meetings. The skills in this chapter have been used successfully with students at all grade levels.

## "How Is That a Problem for You?"

Sometimes it's enough to ask students the following question when their problem comes up on the agenda: "How is that a problem for you?" When they answer, it often becomes obvious to them what *they* could do to improve the situation, without using brainstorming time to help them figure it out. This approach is especially useful with children who do a lot of tattling.

Eight-year-old Joey was bothered by two girls whispering next to him, so he put the issue on the agenda. The teacher asked, "How is this a problem for you?" Joey replied, "I can't get my work done because they're too noisy." The teacher asked Joey if he had any ideas about what he could do to improve the situation. He thought for a minute and said, "I could move and do my work somewhere else, or I could ask them to stop talking." The teacher asked, "Do you still want help with this problem from the class?" "I think I've worked it out," said Joey.

When going through the items on the agenda, asking "Is this still a problem for you?" may eliminate taking class meeting time to work on issues that have already been resolved.

## Talking Versus Fixing

Some issues are too emotional or too complex to be solved at one class meeting. If you think the class may be ganging up on someone, or if the class is blaming instead of searching for solutions, it might be helpful to tell the group that this is one of those issues where "talk time" is needed instead of "fix time." If talking doesn't help, the issue can be put back on the agenda for more discussion at the next meeting, or until it feels appropriate to work on a solution. A cooling-off period may be needed before the issue can be discussed respectfully.

Trying again after a cooling-off period is only an option when the problem is one that is appropriate for the class to solve. If you know that you'll never agree with the students or that they are trying to change something against school policy that is nonnegotiable, be honest with them. Let them know they can brainstorm about how to cope with the situation instead of trying to change it.

## Mistakes as Opportunities for Learning

Sometimes students don't put items on the agenda. This may be because they think others will think less of them if they can't solve problems alone. They might also believe they are supposed to be "perfect," and that putting an issue on the agenda would be a statement that they are "imperfect." If you think this may be the case, it's time to teach your students about mistakes.

We often ask teachers what they were taught about mistakes during their childhood. Ask your students a similar question. See if their answers are like the ones we get:

> Mistakes are bad.
>
> You shouldn't make mistakes.
>
> You are stupid, bad, inadequate, or a failure if you make mistakes.
>
> If you make a mistake, don't let people find out. If they do, make up an excuse even if it isn't true.

Explain that these are "crazy notions" about mistakes, because they not only damage self-esteem, they invite depression and discouragement. It is difficult to learn and grow when we feel discouraged.

Remind your students that we all know people who have made mistakes and then dug themselves into a hole trying to cover them up. We also know that people can be forgiving when others admit their mistakes, apologize, and try to solve the problems they have created.

Teachers have an opportunity to help students change misguided notions about mistakes. Point out that every person in the world will continue to make mistakes as long as he or she lives. Because this is true, it is healthier to see mistakes as opportunities to learn instead of statements

> **Mistakes are
> wonderful opportunities
> to learn.**

Figure 9.1

of inadequacy. Teach kids that when the whole class really understands that we *learn* by making mistakes, they will not mind having their names put on the agenda. Instead they'll see it as an opportunity to get valuable help from their classmates. They'll actually learn to be proud to take responsibility for what they've done, even if it was a mistake, because they know it doesn't mean they are bad or will get in trouble. It means they are willing to be accountable—a necessary step to using mistakes as an opportunity to learn.

Hiding mistakes keeps us isolated; we can't fix mistakes that are hidden, nor can we learn from them. Trying to prevent mistakes keeps us rigid and fearful. Good judgment comes from experience, and experience comes from poor judgment. Ask for a volunteer to make the poster in Figure 9.1 to encourage this new way of thinking about mistakes.

Sometimes mistakes require us to make amends where possible, or at least to apologize. When students learn about the Three Rs of Recovery, they have a tool to use that takes the guilt, shame, and blame out of mistakes.[1]

---

[1] For more information about the Three Rs of Recovery, see Jane Nelsen and Lynn Lott, *I'm on Your Side: Resolving Conflict with Your Teenage Son or Daughter* (Rocklin, CA: Prima Publishing, 1991) and Jane Nelsen, Riki Intner, and Lynn Lott, *Clean and Sober Parenting* (Rocklin, CA: Prima Publishing, 1992).

## The Three Rs of Recovery

Inform your students that making mistakes isn't as important as what we do about them. Anyone can make mistakes,
but it takes a secure person to say, "I'm sorry." If a student
would like to make amends for a mistake, the Three Rs
of Recovery can help them do so. Write these steps on the
board for your students:

1. *Recognize* the mistake with a feeling of responsibility instead of blame.
2. *Reconcile* by apologizing to the people you have of-
   fended or hurt.
3. *Resolve* the problem, when possible, by working
   together on a solution.

Ask the kids if they can think of a time when they made
a mistake and could have used the Three Rs. You may wish
to tell the following story about how a group of seventh-
grade boys dealt with a mistake they made.

Mary was a student who had few friends and spent
a lot of time in the counselor's office instead of with her
classmates. One day she put an item on the agenda concerning her grade. One of the boys blurted out, "Why don't
you try studying for a change!" Two other boys laughed.
Mary appeared hurt by their comments. She turned her
chair around and, although she didn't leave the room, she
refused to continue the discussion. The teacher said, "I
can see Mary is feeling hurt. Boys, are you willing to use
the Three Rs of Recovery? You may not have meant to hurt
her feelings, but sometimes that happens whether we intend it or not."

All three boys in unison said, "Sorry, Mary. We weren't
trying to hurt your feelings. We really do wish you'd pay
more attention to your work so you could do better in

class." Mary inched her chair a little closer to the circle but kept her back to the class. "Mary," said the boy who made the comment, "we made a mistake and we're sorry. We hope you won't stay angry with us." Mary left her chair in place but murmured, "It's okay."

The teacher then asked, "How many of you hate it when your feelings are hurt?" Half the class raised hands. "And what makes you feel better when that happens?" Some of the answers were, "I like it when the person apologizes." "I like it if someone walks with me so we can talk about it." "I like it if someone gives me a hug."

The teacher suggested that after the class meeting, some of the students might do some of those things for Mary. After class, several students went up to talk to Mary and give her a hug. A meeting like this might change how students treat one another, while helping Mary learn behaviors that invite friendship.

## Encouragement Instead of Praise and Rewards

Rudolf Dreikurs, an Adlerian psychologist and author of *Children: The Challenge,* said, "Children need encouragement like a plant needs water."[2] Encouragement is a process of showing the kind of love that conveys to kids that they are good enough the way they are. Encouragement tells kids that what they do is separate from who they are, and it lets them know they are valued for their uniqueness without judgment. Through encouragement we can teach that mistakes are simply opportunities to learn and grow instead of something to be ashamed of. Kids who feel encouraged also gain self-love and a sense of belonging.

[2]Rudolf Dreikurs, *Children: The Challenge* (New York: E. P. Dutton, 1987), p. 36.

If your students are having trouble coming up with nonpunitive and encouraging solutions to problems on the agenda, it may be time to teach them the difference between praise and encouragement. It's easy to praise or reward students who are behaving well, but what can we say to those who are misbehaving and not feeling good about themselves? These are the ones who need encouragement the most.

Use the following example to demonstrate the need for encouragement. What would they say to a student who got *A*s and *B*s on his report card? They might respond, "You're doing so well. You must feel very good about that. You're really smart." What would they say if that same student earned only *D*s and *F*s? He still needs supportive feedback, but it's a lot harder to think of positive things to say.

Ask the class if they would like to learn how to use encouragement instead of praise and to see how encouragement works even when a person is failing. Point out that praise and rewards teach kids to depend on the external judgments of others instead of trusting their internal wisdom and self-evaluation. A steady diet of praise and rewards inspires them to believe, "I'm okay only if others say I'm okay." It also teaches them to avoid mistakes instead of to learn from their mistakes. Put up the "Praise and Encouragement" chart to show more about the differences between praise and encouragement.

After looking at the chart together, go back to the example of the student who is getting *D*s and *F*s and see if the class can think of things they could say or do that would be encouraging. Following are some examples.

"How do you feel about your grades?"

"What happened? Do you have any idea why your grades are dropping?"

| Differences Between Praise and Encouragement[3] | | |
|---|---|---|
| | **Praise** | **Encouragement** |
| **Dictionary Definition** | 1. To express a favorable *judgment* of<br>2. To glorify, especially by attribution of *perfection*<br>3. An expression of *approval* | 1. To inspire with courage<br>2. To spur on: *stimulate* |
| Recognizes | Only complete, perfect product | Effort and improvement |
| Attitude | Patronizing, manipulative | Respectful, appreciative |
| "I" message | Judgmental: "I like the way you are sitting." | Self-disclosing: "I appreciate your cooperation." |
| Used most often with | Children: "You're such a good little girl." | Adults: "Thanks for helping." |
| Examples | "I'm proud of you for getting an *A* in math." (robs person of ownership of own achievement) | "That *A* reflects your hard work." (recognizes ownership and responsibility for achievement) |
| Invites | People to change for others | People to change for themselves |
| Locus of control | External: "What do you think?" | Internal: "What do I think?" |
| Teaches | What to think | How to think |
| Goal | Conformity: "You did it right." | Understanding: "What do you think/feel/learn?" |
| Effect on self-esteem | Feel worthwhile only when others approve | Feel worthwhile without the approval of others |
| Long-range effect | Dependence on others | Self-confidence, self-reliance |

[3]This chart is based on a chart by parent educators and parenting class leaders Bonnie G. Smith and Judy Dixon, Sacramento, CA.

"Would you like some help improving your grades? I'd be happy to help you with your spelling words."

"Hey, anyone can have a bad report card. We still like you a lot."

"I bet you're feeling scared to show this to your parents. Can I walk home with you when you bring them your report card?"

Following are two fun class-meeting activities that encourage discouraged students. Pick a student who needs encouragement. Have him or her sit in the center of the circle, and let students go around the circle taking turns saying an encouraging statement to the student. Or, ask the kids if they would like to practice encouragement by writing notes of encouragement to each other. They could pick a different student for each day, so that each student eventually gets notes of encouragement.

The class may also choose to have the teacher assign students partners for the week. Each pair watches for encouraging things to say and do for each other. It is also each student's responsibility to have a compliment ready for the partner once or twice a week during the class meeting.

Encouragement goes a long way in establishing a positive classroom and class-meeting atmosphere. The students will catch the spirit and will probably come up with other ways to practice encouragement in the classroom. *Encourage* them to do so!

## Routines

Routines establish a sense of order and stability. Life is easier for everyone when there is a smooth rhythm to events in the day. A routine is something students can learn to count on; the routine itself becomes the "boss," and you avoid having teachers or students dictating what will happen. It makes more sense to students to say, "It's time for spelling," than to say, "I need you to do your spelling now." The first statement implies that the teacher is asking the students to check the routine and see what needs to be done, while the second suggests that the teacher should be controlling. Many students feel rebellious when told what to do, but they'd gladly do what needs to be done.

Setting up routines works especially well for scheduling class job times, deciding how materials will get distributed and collected, establishing the way students enter and leave a room and line up for recess in elementary school, and for following procedures outside the classroom, such as assembly, field trips, and using the library. The class meeting is the perfect place to set up routines with your students.

### Six Guidelines for Setting Up Routines

You can create routines that are predictable, consistent, and respectful to all by following the Six Guidelines for Setting Up Routines. Use these guidelines while working with your students during class meetings:

1. Focus on one issue at a time.

2. Discuss the issue when everyone is calm, rather than during a time of conflict.

3. Involve students in developing a routine. Ask for their ideas. If they can't think of any ideas, use limited choices. For instance, ask your students whether they prefer to do math first or English first, or whether they'd like to have their art period

before lunch or at the end of the day. We talk more about limited choices in Chapter 10.

4. Use visuals, such as charts and lists. After the students agree on the order that things will be done, the teacher or one of the students can make a chart itemizing the routines. When it's time for reading, you can ask your students, "What is next on our schedule?" The schedule becomes the boss instead of the teacher.

5. Rehearse through role playing. Have the class pretend that it's time for the chosen activity, and go through a dry run so that everyone knows what's expected.

6. Follow through in a firm and kind manner. Once a routine is established, follow it faithfully. If a student questions or ignores a previously made agreement, ask, "What was our agreement?" Allow the student to experience natural or logical consequences, but not punishment. Resist rescuing and lecturing.

Establishing routines yields long-range benefits of security, a calmer atmosphere, and trust. They also help students develop life skills. They learn to be responsible for their own behavior, to feel capable, and to cooperate in the classroom.

Remember to be realistic and to understand that routines may not work perfectly at first. Students who are used to behaving in certain ways need time before they'll believe that their teachers mean what they say. Remind your students that it's part of human nature to resist change, even when we know it's good for us. It is important to continue to follow the planned routine until their resistance disappears.

## Classroom Jobs

Assigning classroom jobs—giving them opportunities to contribute in meaningful ways—is one of the best methods of helping kids feel belonging and significance. Not only do kids feel better about themselves when they have a job, the teacher doesn't have to *do* everything!

A simple method for assigning classroom jobs is to brainstorm enough jobs so that every student has one. Suggest that at least one of the jobs be Job Monitor, the person who checks the list each day to see if each job got done, and, if it didn't, to remind the student who forgot.

Post the list of jobs on a Job Chart located in a convenient place. Some of the jobs might include the following:

Make job chart

Pass out papers

Collect papers

Feed fish

Water plants

Decorate bulletin board

Decorate room

Straighten bookshelves

Window monitor

Restock supplies

Empty pencil sharpener

Office message monitor

Line monitor

Lunchroom monitor

Playground equipment monitor

Set up a rotation, and switch jobs each week. Sometimes students will prefer to keep the same job for a semester. You may wish to set aside part of each day as job time, so that students aren't disruptive when doing their chores. Some jobs may require training, so take time to show a student where the supplies are or how to succeed at the job. Be available at job time to help students who need your assistance.

## Student Involvement

That's the secret—student involvement. The notion that teachers are isolated in a classroom can end when teachers use the class meeting as a way to use the valuable resources that surround them—capable young people. Student involvement is the secret to cooperation, collaboration, and healthy self-esteem for everyone in the classroom.

# Classroom-Management Tools

Kids learn best—both academic and social skills—when classroom management is based on mutual respect. This chapter provides twelve tools to ensure respectful classroom management throughout the day.

## 1. Limited Choices

Many difficult problems seem easier to solve when choices appear. As the teacher, you can help your students succeed by offering them a choice between at least two acceptable options. The key words are *appropriate* and *acceptable*.

Many times a choice is not *appropriate*. It's not appropriate, for instance, to give students a choice about whether or not they want to learn to read, go to school, hurt someone else, be in a dangerous situation such as climbing on the roof, and so on. Examples of appropriate limited choices are: "You may read this book or this other book." "It's not okay to hurt your classmate. You can apologize now, or take some time to cool off and put this on the agenda for the next class meeting." "You may stay at recess if you stay off the school roof. If you can't handle that, you can return to the classroom and try again tomorrow."

It's not *appropriate* to give broad choices to young kids, such as, "Where do you want to sit?" or "What do you want to learn?" They need more limited choices, such as, "You may sit at this table or that table," or "We can do our art assignment first or our math assignment. Which do you prefer?" As they get older, the choices you give them can be much broader, because their skills at making decisions and dealing with consequences, will be better developed. With young students you might say, "Would you like to write a report on a butterfly or turtle?" With older students you could give a choice, such as, "Would you like one week or two weeks to get your report done? You pick the topic."

A choice is *acceptable* when you are willing to accept either option the student chooses. Don't offer a choice that is not acceptable to you.

## 2. Four Problem-Solving Steps

Often difficulties arise in the classroom that can be easily handled outside the class meeting yet still allow the students, rather than the teacher, to take responsibility for their behavior. Such problems might be solvable by using the Four Problem-Solving Steps. Introduce these steps to the class early in the year, and post them in the room.

    1. Ignore it.

    2. Talk it over respectfully with the other student.

3. Agree with the other student on a solution.

4. Put it on the class-meeting agenda.

Step 1 encourages students to avoid involvement or to leave the area of conflict for a cooling-off period. Step 2 is an opportunity for students to tell each other how they feel, to listen to and respect their own feelings, to figure out what they did to contribute to the problem, and tell the other person what they are willing to do differently. Step 3 could involve working out a win/win solution together or else apologizing. Step 4 lets students know it's okay to ask for help.

When students come to you with a problem, refer them to the Four Problem-Solving Steps chart, and ask if they have tried any of the steps. If they haven't tried any, ask which one they would like to try. This keeps you out of the "fix-it" role.

## 3. Follow-Through

When it's not appropriate to wait for a class meeting to solve a problem, a teacher can decide what to do and can follow through with kind and firm action instead of lectures or punishment. When you use ten words or less that stick to the issue, you avoid lecturing. (One word or a pantomimed gesture is best.)

For example, Mrs. Adams was having a hard time with Justin, who continuously got out of his seat to ask her questions all day long. Although she tried to answer his questions, she noticed he really seemed to want constant attention. Mrs. Adams tuned into her feelings of irritation and used the Mistaken Goal Chart (See Appendix C) to verify that Justin's goal was Undue Attention. This helped her decide on a plan to encourage him. She said to Justin, "I notice you have a lot of questions. I'm willing to answer three a day. I'll hold up my fingers each time I answer a question, and when three fingers are used up, I won't answer any more questions until tomorrow. You might want to make sure you can't figure out the answer for yourself before you ask me." In this way, Mrs. Adams was weaning Justin from undue attention, but still giving him some special attention with their "private" signal.

Justin acted in his old way on Monday, and Mrs. Adams followed through with firmness and kindness, and no words, after she had answered three questions. On Tuesday he came up to Mrs. Adams' desk twice as many times as usual. (Kids often try harder at first to get the response they used to get before they find a new way of behaving.) She wondered if her idea was going to work, but she remembered that she had decided to try following through for one week. When Justin whined because Mrs. Adams wouldn't answer any more questions, she smiled at him and held up her three fingers. By the fourth day he came up twice, and on Friday he said, "I think I'll only have three questions today. That's enough for next week, too."

Mrs. Adams breathed a sigh of relief and said, "Justin, I'm feeling much better about answering your questions when you don't ask so many. I notice you've been finding many answers for yourself. You are doing a good job."

Justin learned that his teacher means what she says and will follow through with firm and kind action. He also learned that his choices have a related, respectful, and reasonable consequence. Justin has a choice of asking twenty questions and getting three answered or asking three questions. He is learning about responsibility. He is also learning that he's capable of finding some answers for himself. One of the greatest gifts for Justin is the opportunity to learn about treating himself and others with dignity and respect, which the teacher so beautifully demonstrates.

Follow-through takes less energy and is much more fun and productive than scolding, lecturing, and punishing. Follow-through helps teachers be proactive and thoughtful instead of reactive and inconsiderate. Follow-through can help you empower students by respecting who they are while teaching them the importance of making a contribution to the classroom. It is an excellent alternative to authoritarian methods or permissiveness. With follow-through you can *meet the needs of the situation* while maintaining dignity and respect for all concerned. Follow-through is one way to help children learn the life skills they need to feel good about themselves while learning to be contributing members of society.

When children are younger (toddlers to age eight), follow-through is relatively simple. When you say something, mean it. When you mean it, follow through with kindness and firmness. Or, as Dreikurs used to say to parents and teachers, "Shut your mouth and act."

Mrs. Valdez was in the habit of coaxing Jennifer to put her blocks away and come to the reading circle. After learning about follow-through, she decided on a different course of action. The next day at reading time, she went over to Jennifer, took her by the hand, and kindly and firmly led her to the circle. Just before recess Mrs. Valdez asked Jennifer, "What do you need to do before you'll be ready for recess?" Jennifer innocently said, "I don't know." Mrs. Valdez simply pointed to the blocks. Jennifer went over to the blocks and dallied. She had about half the blocks picked up when the recess bell rang. Mrs. Valdez stopped her at the door, led her back to the block area, and pointed at the blocks. Jennifer picked them up as fast as she could so she wouldn't miss any more recess.

113

Jennifer learned that her manipulative tactics were no longer effective. Mrs. Valdez learned how much easier and effective it is to follow through with very few words than it is to use lectures, threats, and punishment.

## Four Steps for Effective Follow-Through

Follow-through is more effective and teaches more skills as children get older and more involved in the process of solving problems and making agreements. The Four Steps for Effective Follow-Through describe this process:

1. Have a friendly discussion where everyone (during a class meeting or during a conference with one or more students) gets to voice his or her feelings and thoughts about an issue.

2. Brainstorm for possible solutions, and choose one with which both the teacher and the student or students agree.

3. Agree on a specific time deadline (to the minute).

4. Understand your students well enough to know that the deadline may not be met, and simply follow through with your part of the agreement by holding them accountable, as in the above example.

If you think your students won't cooperate as readily as Justin and Jennifer did, don't be discouraged. If you follow the Four Steps to Effective Follow-Through and avoid the Four Traps That Defeat Effective Follow-Through given below, students will cooperate, even when they don't especially want to. They seem to pick up the feeling that what is required is reasonable, and that they are being held accountable respectfully.

## Four Traps That Defeat Effective Follow-Through

1. Expecting kids to have the same priorities as adults.

2. Judging and criticizing instead of sticking to the issue.

3. Not getting (noncoerced) agreements in advance that include a specific deadline or specific action the teacher will take.

4. Not maintaining dignity and respect for the student and yourself.

As you reread the examples with Justin and Jennifer, you'll see that the teacher avoided all the traps that defeat effective follow-through.

Some teachers object to follow-through, saying, "We don't want to have to remind students to keep their agreements. We expect them to be responsible without any reminders from us." We have three questions for these teachers: (1) When you don't take time to remind them with dignity and respect, do you spend time scolding, lecturing, and punishing them for not keeping their agreements? (2) Have you noticed how responsible kids are about keeping agreements that are important to them? (3) Do you really think Jennifer would rather read than play with the blocks? (Even though reading may not be her priority, it is important that she learn to read.)

Follow-through is a gentle way to guide kids to do what needs to be done for their greater benefit, or to maintain respect for self and others. Raising or teaching children is not easy. Follow-through *can* make it easier— and rewarding, too.

## 4. Ask, Don't Tell
## "What," "Why," and "How"[1]

Too many teachers *tell* students what happened, why it happened, how they should feel about it, and what they should do about it instead of *asking* them what happened, what is their perception of why it happened, how they feel about it, and how they could use that information next time.

When we *tell* instead of *ask,* we discourage students from developing their judgment skills, consequential skills, and accountability skills. We fail to give them the wonderful gift of seeing mistakes as opportunities to learn. Telling instead of asking also teaches them *what* to think instead *how* to think, which is very dangerous in a society filled with peer pressure, cults, and gangs. Whenever you are tempted to *tell,* stop yourself and *ask.*

An eighth-grade teacher wanted to rearrange her room. She started to tell the students what to do and suddenly realized that this would be a great opportunity for them to think through the steps on their own. She asked, "Do you have any ideas for how we could arrange the room so everyone can see each other?" Five or six students had suggestions, and the class voted to choose one of the ideas.

Out of habit, the teacher started to instruct everyone on what to do and realized again, that she could ask instead of telling. It took a lot longer to rearrange the room, but the kids got practice in thinking and in being actively involved. Although she was aware of how difficult it is to

[1]For more information, see H. Stephen Glenn and Jane Nelsen, *Raising Self-Reliant Children in a Self-Indulgent World* (Rocklin, CA: Prima Publishing, 1989), and Jane Nelsen and H. Stephen Glenn, *Time Out* (Fair Oaks, CA: Sunrise Press, 1991). Pages 68–72 include an article by a high school principal, Kent Mann, who developed a system based on what, why, and how questions for working with students sent to his office for behavior problems. Both books are also available from Sunrise Books, Tapes, and Videos, 1-800-456-7770.

break the habit of giving all the instructions instead of asking questions, she decided it's worth working on, because her students became more engaged than usual, and they all pitched in to move the room instead of leaving the job for a few "regulars."

## 5. Redirection Questions

One of the best ways to redirect behavior is through asking questions related to the behavior you would like to change. For example, when the class is getting too noisy, ask, "How many of you think it's too noisy for people to concentrate? How many do not?" It's important to ask the question both ways in order to allow room for honest responses.

Asking the question is usually enough to invite the students to think about their behavior and what needs to be done. When an atmosphere of mutual respect has been established, the students usually want to cooperate. The question simply helps them become aware of what's needed.

Ask the question while the students keep working. No discussion is needed, but it's interesting to watch how much the situation improves just by asking a redirection question. We watched one teacher use a creative variation of a redirection question by stopping the class in the middle of an activity and saying, "I just have to ask, how many of you want to help Jose with his times tables? Jose, look at all those hands! Pick someone to help you practice your 7s."

## 6. Doing Nothing (Natural Consequences)

Surprisingly, an effective tool for mutually respectful classroom management is to do nothing and watch to see what happens. An eighth-grade math teacher responded to every little interruption in her classroom. She answered every question, commented on every annoyance, and spent most of her class time putting out fires and getting nowhere. When she heard about the do-nothing idea, she was shocked. It had never occurred to her that she could let some things go by, but she decided to try this new approach.

To her surprise, students usually stopped the disturbing behavior, or classmates asked them to stop. The numerous questions seemed to disappear when she stopped responding to the ones that seemed inappropriate. Later she overheard a student saying, "Don't ask teacher. She's having a bad day. Maybe I can answer that question."

When she heard the students helping each other, she said, "I'm so happy to see how much you can handle without my involvement. I'm not angry with you or having a bad day, but I really would like to do less responding and more teaching. How many are willing to help me out?" The entire class raised their hands.

## 7. Deciding What to Do Instead of Trying to Control Others

Will we ever learn that the only behavior we can control is our own? Adults may be able to make children *act* respectfully, but we can't make them *feel* respectful. The best way to encourage them to *feel* respectful is to control our own behavior and be a model of respect for ourselves and others.

We are disrespectful to kids when we try to control their behavior. An important part of respect and encouragement is honoring a person's right to control his or her own behavior. Even though adults are often disrespectful to children, they insist that children show respect to adults. Does this make sense? Be a model of respect in order to teach respect.

Deciding what to do instead of trying to control others may be a new thought for some teachers. Many teachers have been so busy trying to control their students that they haven't considered the many possibilities for dealing with problems by controlling their own behavior and deciding what they'll do themselves. The following examples should start you thinking creatively.

One teacher got tired of repeating directions all the time. She told the class that she would give directions only once and, if necessary, write them on the board. If someone didn't understand or hear the directions, that was okay; that student could ask a classmate. The teacher was not going to repeat herself. Some students still came to her, but when they did, she simply smiled and shrugged her shoulders. The kids would either begin working or ask others for help.

Another way to decide what you'll do is to make an agreement with a student based on what you are willing to do. For example, you might tell a student, "I'll be available for tutoring every Thursday afternoon from 3:00 to 3:15. If you want my help, I'll be there." If the student doesn't show up and then wants help at a time that is inconvenient for you, say something like "I'll be available again at 3:00 next Thursday."

At their first class meeting, one seventh-grade class organized the room by putting the tables in a circle and sitting on top of them, even though it was against the teacher's rules. They swung their legs throughout the meeting. Later an aide asked the teacher why she let the students sit on the tables, since it was against the rules. She also wondered if the leg swinging wasn't driving the teacher crazy. The teacher replied that she had decided to watch and wait and see if the arrangement created a prob-lem. Even though the leg swinging was a bit annoying, she noticed that the important work was getting done; the students were working on problem solving together, and the meeting proceeded without a hitch. She decided that the leg swinging would not be an issue if she didn't make it one. By the end of the meeting, she didn't even notice whether the kids were still swinging their legs.

## 8. Saying No with Dignity and Respect

It's okay to say no. If all you *ever* say is no, that's a prob-lem, but some teachers don't think they have the right to say no without lengthy explanations.

One day when a group of students were feeling especially rowdy in a sixth-grade class, they asked their teacher, "Can we take a break and play a game?" The teacher responded, "No." "Why not? That's not fair. Mr. Smith lets his class do it."

This time the teacher said, "Watch my lips. [No]." "Aw come on, be a sport. You're so tight." "What part of 'No' don't you understand?" "Okay. You're no fun. I guess we have to finish our work." The teacher just smiled.

## 9. Acting More, Talking Less

You can act, instead of talk. Listen to yourself for one day. You might be amazed at how many useless words you speak! If you decide to act more and talk less, your students will begin to notice the difference. Instead of asking the class to be quiet over and over, wait quietly for them to give you their attention. Flip a light switch if it gets too noisy. One teacher, who constantly nagged her students to stay away from the blackboard when they came into the room, started walking over to them with her lips closed, gently removing the chalk from their hands, and softly turning them toward their desk. The kids were so shocked, they sat down immediately and opened their books and got started working. The teacher was almost as shocked as the kids.

She learned to stop saying things she didn't mean. If she meant it, she was prepared to follow through with action instead of words. Since that meant giving an issue her full attention from start to finish, she soon began to ignore minor interruptions and dealt with the ones that were really important.

## 10. Putting Everyone in the Same Boat

Teachers often pick on one student instead of putting everyone in the same boat. It's difficult to really know all the players involved and to pretend to have the ability to be judge, jury, and prosecutor all at once. Some applications of this idea may sound like the following:

> One or two students are whispering while others are doing their work: "Kids, it's too noisy in here."

> Someone tattles on another student: "I'm sure you kids can work it out."

> A student grabs another student's book, and papers fly all over the room: "Kids, please pick up the papers and get back to work."

If the class responds with, "That's not fair. I wasn't doing anything wrong," or "Teacher, it was Tom, not me," simply say, "I'm not interested in finding fault or pointing fingers but in getting the problem resolved."

121

Another problem is that many teachers think it's *their* job to fix everything, and that *they* are the only ones with good ideas. Another variation of putting kids in the same boat is to ask the kids to figure out what to do, and watch their creativity at work.

In one classroom the students were fighting over who got to use the balls at recess. The teacher said, "I'm putting the balls away until you kids figure out a system for sharing without fighting. Let me know when you've worked it out, and you can try again." At first the students grumbled, but later three boys announced, "We worked it out. The kids whose last names start with A through M can have the balls on Mondays and Wednesdays, and the N through Z kids can have them on Tuesdays and Thursdays. Friday is free day. We all agreed."

If the students start squabbling again, the teacher can simply say, "Back to the drawing board. The ball-sharing plan seems to be falling apart. Let me know when you're ready to try again, and you can use the balls."

## II. Positive Time Out[2]

Time out can be a positive tool—an encouraging and empowering experience for students instead of being punitive and humiliating. Time out is encouraging when the purpose is to give students a chance to take a break for a short time and try again as soon as they're ready to change their behavior. We all have times when, for one reason or another, we don't feel like doing what's required and may chose some form of acting out instead. Time out can be a *cooling-off period.*

[2]See also Jane Nelsen and H. Stephen Glenn, *Time Out* (Fair Oaks, CA: Sunrise Press, 1991), also available from Sunrise Books, Tapes, and Videos, 1-800-456-7770.

Teachers see the value of encouraging time out when they are more concerned with long-range benefits to students than with short-term control at the expense of students. Punitive time out may stop misbehavior for the moment, but the benefits are only short-term if the student decides to get even or give up. The key to encouraging positive time out is the attitude of the teacher and the explanation given to students.

Explain to students that everyone needs time out once in a while, because we all misbehave and make mistakes at times. It can help to have a place to sort out feelings, calm down, and then make a decision about what to do. Feelings and actions are not the same. What we feel is never inappropriate. What we do often is. "If your behavior is inappropriate (disrespectful to others), I may ask you to go to the time-out area. This is not meant for punishment, but for a time to calm down until you feel better. As soon as you feel better (and you can decide when that is), you can rejoin the group." (Some teachers provide a timer for students to set according to how much time they think they'll need to feel better.)

Kids *do* better when they *feel* better. We don't motivate kids to do better by making them feel worse through punitive time out. It does *not* help to tell students, "Go to time out and think about what you did." It *is* helpful to tell students, "When you are in time out, do something to help you feel better. You may want to read a book, take a short nap, think about your favorite things, or just gaze out the window."

Teachers are often afraid students will take advantage of such an invitation. If they do, you have another problem that needs attention: a power struggle or revenge cycle. You may need to follow any of the suggestions on the Mistaken Goal Chart (see Appendix C); ask what, why, and how questions; or get help during a class meeting for solutions.

Some schools call the time-out bench the "happy bench." When students are misbehaving on the playground, yard supervisors will say, "Go to the happy bench until you feel better and are ready to do better."

## 12. Taking Small Steps

Taking small steps is an important classroom management tool. The road to success is one step at a time. If you set your sights too high, you may never start, or you may feel discouraged if everything doesn't happen overnight. If you continue taking small steps, you will move forward, and you and your students will all benefit.

The point of nonpunitive classroom management tools is to teach students that mistakes are opportunities to learn, to give them life skills that will serve them when adults are not around, and to help them feel belonging and significance so they don't feel a need to engage in nonproductive behavior.

# Questions and Answers About Class Meetings

**A**s you experience class meetings, many questions will arise. Here are answers to some of the most frequently asked questions from hundreds of teachers. Some questions are from elementary school teachers and some from junior high and high school teachers. Even though there are some developmental differences between students of different ages, there are many similarities. Teachers of all grade levels will find creative ideas for solving problems in the answers to all the questions. Watch for the basic principles of respect and empowerment in the answers. Hearing enough solutions based on dignity and respect will stimulate more creativity for empowering students— and yourself.

## Questions Frequently Asked by Elementary School Teachers

**Question:** How do I avoid having students humiliated at a class meeting?

It is important to guide students away from any suggestions that would humiliate or hurt another student. Several questions help: "How would that be helpful for this person?" "How would you feel if that suggestion were given to you?" "Is that humiliating or respectful?" "Does that punish for past behavior or encourage change for future behavior?" Is the punishment related, respectful, and reasonable?

Humiliation and punishment can be avoided by having the student with the problem choose the solution that would be the most helpful. Sometimes students do choose punitive solutions for themselves. To help them get out of the punitive mentality, you might ask, "How will that help and encourage you?"

Another way to avoid humiliation is through generalizing. This means talking about the issue in general terms instead of a specific problem involving a specific child. Suppose, for example, someone uses the agenda to accuse another person of stealing. This issue might be generalized by brainstorming for solutions. Ask the class, "What can we do to deal with the problem of stealing in general, instead of looking for blame and trying to control one person?"

Another way to handle a situation when you perceive that humiliation is taking place is to ask redirection questions: "How many of you would feel helped if you were in Johnny's place right now? How many of you would not?" "How many of you would feel ganged up on? How many would not?"

126

Generalization and redirection will be needed less often when kids catch on to the spirit of helping, rather than hurting and punishing, one another.

**Question:** Don't students get resentful when they ask for help and you tell them to put it on the class meeting agenda instead of helping them right away?

Actually, most students feel immediate relief just by putting their problem on the agenda. Many do feel resentful because they are used to special attention from the teacher. Others are used to being taken care of instead of being involved in the helping process. Change (even for the good) is not always easy. Some may feel resentful at first, but not after they experience the positive attention and help they can receive during class meetings, which is usually much more creative than the help they receive from teachers.

A second-grade student complained to her teacher, Mrs. Binns, that some boys were kicking her seat on the bus. Mrs. Binns suggested she put that problem on the agenda and ask the kids for help. The first suggestion was profoundly simple: "Sit in back of them." A creatively complicated suggestion was, "Get on the bus and put your books in one seat, then sit in another seat. When the boys sit behind you, you can move to the seat where your books are." There were many other suggestions, but the student chose the suggestion to watch where the boys sat and sit far away from them. (See Chapter 10 for other suggestions to deal with requests for help.)

**Question:** How many times should students be allowed to put something on the agenda in one day?

Put this question on the agenda and ask the kids. One teacher had been allowing two or three items per person each day, and the issues were endless. He put the question

127

on the agenda, and the students decided on the rule of one item per person each day. There hasn't been a problem since they discussed the issue and made a decision.

**Question:** What do you do if the kids won't pick a suggestion?

Give a limited choice to students who won't choose a suggestion—they must either choose or let the class vote on one. Take, for example, the two boys who were always late from recess. The class brainstormed ideas. Their teacher asked the two boys to choose the one that would be most helpful. One of the boys chose to play closer to the bell. The other boy didn't want to choose any of the suggestions. He was given the option of either choosing one or letting the class vote on one for him. That motivated him to choose playing closer to the bell.

**Question:** Can I use class meetings to deal with problems that happen outside the classroom?

There are two ways to deal with problems occurring outside class. One is to help the person with the problem decide what he or she can do, since it is impossible to control other people. The other way is to invite the other person or people to the class meeting and involve them in the problem-solving process.

It came to Mr. Ryan's attention that some of his students were misbehaving on the school bus. He asked them to pretend they were the bus driver. Then they went around the circle and expressed what they thought it would feel like to be the bus driver and what frustrations and problems they would experience. They went on to talk about some of the problems the bus driver was complaining about on the bus. He didn't want them to play games because he had to wait too long for them to put things away and get off the bus. It was messing up his schedule, because he had to make double runs.

The solution the students came up with was to be allowed to have games on the bus as long as they used them appropriately and put them in their knapsacks before the bus reached the school. They also proposed that if the games were used inappropriately, the bus driver or teacher could confiscate them but would give them a chance to try again in a month.

The kids picked a committee of two to meet with the bus driver in question, tell him they had discussed the problem at their class meeting, inform him of their suggested solution, and ask if he would be willing to try it out. He said, "Yes."

A week later, the bus driver appeared at the class meeting to thank the students for their cooperation. He said he'd had this problem for years, and this was the first time anything worked to solve it.

## Questions Frequently Asked by Junior High and High School Teachers

**Question:** Is it okay to move students who sit next to their friends and create a lot of disturbance at the class meeting?

This problem comes up frequently. Mr. Burke noticed his students had a difficult time being respectful when they were sitting next to their friends. He tried lecturing them about being inconsiderate. When that didn't work, he decided to separate the sets of friends. The kids responded with hostility and resistance to the whole idea of class meetings.

Mr. Burke decided to put the problem on the agenda. He asked his students these questions during a class meeting, and got these responses:

1. What problems do you think we might have when friends sit together? The students brainstormed

129

the likely problems, such as talking, giggling, and passing notes.

2. What suggestions do you have for solving these problems? The students agreed to be respectful so they could have the privilege of sitting with friends.

3. What would be a related, respectful, and reasonable consequence if people don't keep their agreements to be respectful while sitting with a friend? The students decided that being separated from their friends for the rest of that meeting would be a logical consequence if they were disrespectful, but that they would want to be given a chance to try again at the next class meeting.

Predictably, nothing was effective until the students became involved in the problem-solving process. Although they often come to the same conclusions that teachers try to impose on them, the results are totally different.

**Question:** Are sixth-graders too immature for class meetings? The kids in my class act silly, make fun of each other, and sometimes are jerks to each other.

Developmentally, sixth-graders are beginning to respond more to peer influence than to adult influence. They are also wanting to fit in with their classmates, so if negative behavior gets started, it may be difficult to stop.

Students sometimes act silly because teachers start class meetings before they teach the skills. One teacher who was having difficulties told her students she had made a mistake by starting class meetings without teaching more skills. After two months of not doing much more than forming a circle, teaching basic skills, and exchanging compliments, the students settled down and were ready to use problem-solving skills.

**Question:** If the students are uncomfortable or embarrassed exchanging compliments, would it be okay to skip that part of the meeting?

We think the compliment process is extremely important, and that it is best not to let it be an option. Students (and adults) overcome the embarrassment stage of *giving and receiving* compliments when you stick with it. Still, as long as the opening activity is positive and results in the students' learning more about each other so that they can begin to give compliments, variations are possible.

One possibility is to use this time to get to know each other by asking a question about outside interests, special hobbies, or other personal information. One teacher has a special book with thoughts for the day. She passes it around the class meeting and lets each student respond personally to the inspirational message.

**Question:** Any ideas for handling backhanded compliments?

A simple way to handle a backhanded compliment is to say, "Oops, is that a compliment or an agenda item?" Another question that helps redirect a backhanded compliment is, "Would you please rephrase that until it sounds like something you would like to hear?"

**Question:** Isn't it true that some kids just don't need compliments?

"Need" in what way? Compliments may appear to be a luxury, but they pay off in terms of self-esteem and confidence.

A high school teacher teaching advanced physics with a group of students with the reputation of being "nerds," and "brains" said, "If compliments are all you do, class meetings are worth it. Take as long as you need. The kids in my class get so much negative criticism, that compliments at the class meeting was the first time some of them heard anything positive about themselves at school."

**Question:** If I read this book, will that be enough to succeed at class meetings?

Reading this book will be a big help, but teachers who hold class meetings on a regular basis say they have a need for ongoing support. They prefer having an after-school meeting once a month with other teachers where they can encourage and empower each other. Many teachers use the Teachers-Helping-Teachers Problem-Solving Steps (discussed in Appendices A and B) at these meetings, to help them deal with certain problems that benefit from the perspective and support of others. Teachers make excellent consultants to each other. The Teachers-Helping-Teachers Problem-Solving steps provide them with the opportunity to understand their students better through role-playing the problem, and to realize how many respectful solutions there are through brainstorming.

**Question:** Is it really possible to hold class meetings in a school where we have different kids in different groupings at different times of the day? Wouldn't kids get sick of meetings if every teacher had them? A kid might end up at six meetings a day.

The solution to this problem is for an entire school to hold class meetings at the same time. Some schools have a "prep" period or "advisory" period the first part of the day, and that time can be used for class meetings.

When students and teachers are well trained in the class-meeting process, short meetings can be held in other classrooms for problems unique to that class. Short meetings do not work when teachers and students are not familiar with the process.

We watched some students in a middle school participate in three class meetings in one day. They were enthusiastic, not bored. It was exciting for us to watch their skills improve significantly in each class meeting.

**Question:** Can you really accomplish enough if you only meet once a week?

As students get older, they're able to retain class-meeting skills for a longer period of time. For this reason, it can be effective to have class meetings only once a week if longer blocks of time are not possible.

We've talked to counselors in different schools who have been introducing the idea of class meetings to their faculty. They say that for starters, the best they can expect teachers to go along with is a class meeting once a week. They also commented that the success of the meeting is more dependent on the atmosphere created by the teacher than the age of the students.

When teachers start meeting once a week and experience some success, they often want to meet for shorter times more often. In elementary schools, three to five meetings a week cut down on long agendas and help students build skills. Some teachers have shared that the keys to success are daily class meetings. Older students are able to wait longer than elementary school students, but the opportunity to present their concerns and work on solutions at least once a week is important.

A high school math teacher has daily meetings with his basic math students and weekly meetings with his precalculus seniors. The meetings last ten to fifteen minutes, although he allowed twenty minutes at the beginning of the year to go over class-meeting procedures. He schedules them at the end of the hour, because the students often get so involved, the meetings would cut into his lesson plan if he started at the beginning of the period. Although he was concerned that class meetings would take away from academic learning, he found that his students now do better academically. He said, "Either the class meetings are extremely effective, or kids are getting smarter these days. My students resisted when I first started class meetings. Now they don't let me forget them."

**Question:** Sometimes junior high and high school students feel like they're "ratting" to bring up problems about other kids. How do I address this problem?

It helps to talk about how the class meeting is an alternative to suspensions and other "unhelpful" punitive approaches. Remind them that it's normal to feel reluctant to "rat" on someone in a system that focuses on blame and punishment instead of accountability and solutions. Ask, "How many of you would want your name on the agenda if you knew people would gang up on you and try to *get* you?" Then ask, "How many would want your name on the agenda if you knew you would be getting thousands of dollars worth of valuable consultation from your peers that would be encouraging and empowering?"

**Question:** I've noticed a lot of complaints from students about other teachers at our school who are unwilling to hold class meetings. How do I handle this without making the other teachers look bad?

If kids have issues with teachers who won't hold meetings or discuss issues respectfully with them, it's important to help kids focus on what *they can do* to take responsibility to solve their own problems. Remind them that we can't change others, just ourselves. If other teachers are willing, they could attend your meeting as a guest to help work on a problem.

It helps to train all the faculty about class meetings and their potential. Remind them that human growth is about learning, and learning isn't smooth. The ultimate goal is to talk things over respectfully and solve problems. The fringe benefit is that there are fewer discipline problems, and positive motivation improves in classes that have regular class meetings. The more preparation the staff has ahead of time, the better they do with class meetings.

**Question:** Do I really need an agenda?

Yes. The agenda serves as a powerful, symbolic message that all students have the opportunity to voice their concerns while giving and receiving encouragement and practical help. The agenda also keeps you out of the middle. As we've mentioned before, as issues come up during the week, ask the students to put them on the agenda.

**Question:** What if students choose a poor solution?

If the class agrees on a solution and later realizes it was a mistake, bring it up at the next meeting and work out another solution. On some occasions you may say, "I can't live with that one." It's best to avoid saying this often, because kids learn so much more by trying out a "bad" suggestion (if it isn't humiliating to another student) for a day or a week and discovering for themselves that it's not a respectful or workable idea. Another possibility is to role-play the chosen solution, asking the players if they think the suggestion would really help after they've had a chance to experience seeing the solution in action.

**Question:** What are some of the most common problems found on the agenda at the high school level?

Usually, at the high school level the class meeting is used to solve problems between the teacher and the students. The students really appreciate the chance to give input and work with the teacher on a solution. Some of the most common agenda items include: (1) sitting where they want; (2) no homework on weekends; (3) getting off task (the teacher brings this one up); (4) too much talking; (5) having a hard time paying attention to the teacher after working in small groups; (6) wasting time; and (7) students not showing respect for others.

The problem itself is not of primary importance. Problems provide the opportunity to create a nurturing atmosphere where students can be empowered with the courage, confidence, and skills they need to be productive, contributing, and happy citizens of the world. When you have this long-range perspective, you won't be discouraged by the ups and downs of class meetings. You may have a lousy class meeting one week and a great one the next. Isn't that what life is all about? What better way to teach kids effective ways to handle their own lives!

## CHAPTER

## 12

# Summary of a Question-and-Answer Session

This is a partial transcript of the question-and-answer session during an all-day in-service for 500 teachers presented by Jane Nelsen in Charlotte, North Carolina. A special part of this workshop was the participation of first-grade teacher Janice Ritter and fourth-grade teacher Kay Rogers, who answered questions about class meetings. Jane visited Janice's and Kay's classrooms several months before the workshop and was thrilled to see students and teachers working together to create an atmosphere of mutual respect—kids were helping each other solve problems and learn life skills, and teachers were giving up their disciplinary hassles.[1]

[1] The complete session is part of the six-cassette series entitled *Positive Discipline in the Classroom Featuring Class Meetings,* available from Sunrise Books, Tapes, and Videos, 1-800-456-7770.

*Jane Nelsen:* Today I have with me two teachers from Sharon School. I'd like them to introduce themselves and tell just a little bit about their experience.

*Janice Ritter:* Last year, when we first started class meetings, my initial reaction was, "Well, this is a terrific idea, but it's not going to fly with first-graders." I didn't think they could come up with a compliment, let alone solve problems. I went ahead and began the class-meeting process the first week of school, and by December I said, "This is the most wonderful thing that has ever happened to me as a teacher and for the students."

I would like to share a few reasons why I like using class meetings. First of all, you have more children telling you what is going on in your classroom. Also, children sometimes take things said by a peer a lot better than they'll take it from you. Children can say things to each other in a way that reaches children. Adults don't do that very well. I also like the academic skills that grow out of class meetings.

*Jane:* I hope you all heard that. Say that again.

*Janice:* The academic skills. As beginning writers, they love to go to that agenda, and it helps their writing skills. I have children who speak in a whisper all day long except when they have something they want to say at the class meeting. Probably the reason I like it the best is because behavior improves.

*Jane:* A lot of teachers start class meetings to help with discipline problems and to improve behavior. That is an extremely valid reason. However, behavior improvement is a fringe benefit. The main benefit is that it teaches children the Significant Seven that you all have on your handouts. [See Chapter 1.] That's the foundation that will help them improve their behavior not only now, but all their lives.

*Kay Rogers:* When our school psychologist gave me a copy of *Positive Discipline* and wanted me to implement class meetings, my initial reaction was, "Oh no. This is another program that I'm going to have to read, and it's not going to work." There is no one here who could have a more negative attitude than I did. I decided to try it anyway, and after one week I was sold.

*Jane:* You didn't have a whole month of hell?

*Kay:* [laughs] No. After one of week of class meetings, it was just wonderful. What it did for me was take care of little nit-picky things that drive teachers crazy. The kids would come to me and say, "Somebody hit me." "Somebody touched me." I would say, "Put it on the agenda." That was what made it worthwhile for me in the beginning. We have worked with class meetings and improved upon them. I have a student teacher who began introducing the idea of Robert's Rules. Not only are they learning problem-solving skills, they are also learning skills that will help them with student government. This has been a tremendous fringe benefit, as well as getting the discipline improved within the classroom.

*Jane:* I heard that the year before you learned class meetings, you were asking the psychologist for a lot of help with problem behaviors. She told me she never hears from you any more, and that when she asks if you need anything, you tell her you and the kids are working things out together.

*Kay:* That's true.

*Jane:* Kay and Janice will now help me answer some of the questions that were turned in by the faculty members from each school.

**Question:** Should we post rules in our classroom? And if so, should these be teacher rules, student rules, or a combination of both?

*Kay:* At the beginning of the year my students and I worked out our own rules together in the classroom. Our school has schoolwide rules, which are also posted in our classroom. They were rules that the student council had come up with.

*Jane:* What did you find when you asked the kids to come up with rules?

*Janet:* My students came up with pretty much the same things adults would come up with.

*Jane:* That's so interesting. I've never been in a classroom yet where there weren't rules posted. But usually they are all neatly printed out by the teacher in advance, so there's no ownership by the kids. What we have found is that the kids will either come up with the same rules or even tougher rules, but then they have ownership and you can label them "We decided" instead of "I decided."

**Question:** Should a kindergarten classroom meeting include an agenda?

*Jane:* We had an experience in Elk Grove School District where a group came to visit Project ACCEPT.[2] They

---

[2]Project ACCEPT (Adlerian Counseling Concepts for Encouraging Parents and Teachers) was a federally funded project directed by Jane Nelsen. The focus of this project was to improve student behavior by training significant adults (parents and teachers) to use Adlerian/ Dreikursian methods with children. The main focus for teachers was the use of class meetings. Parents attended parent-study groups. After three years of developmental status, the project achieved exemplary status and was awarded dissemination funds for three years. During this three-year period, school districts throughout California used adoption funds for training with their school faculties and parents.

were writing a project on decision making and had decided it wasn't possible for kids to get involved in decision making until they were in the second grade. But then they watched our kindergarten and our first-grade classes, and they were amazed! They said, "We've got to go back and rewrite the project." Many kindergarten teachers are relieved not to have to deal with tattletale issues. They just say, "Put that on the agenda." Pretty soon the kids get tired of that broken record, so they just put it on the agenda. Half the time they can't remember what their problem was by the time their name comes up on the agenda.

In kindergarten or first grade it might be okay for children to forget their problems, because once they've had a little time to cool off, it doesn't really matter anyway. But you don't want them to forget too many of their problems, or they won't have the opportunity to work on problem-solving skills.

**Question:** What do you do when the compliments get monotonous? For example, I want to compliment you for being my friend or compliment the same person every day.

*Janice:* When that happens, I've done a few things. It happened in the beginning of this year—they were getting very stale. So one day, instead of doing compliments I said, "Today we're going to tell everyone one thing that we're working on." They went around the room and came up with some really good things that they're working on. Whether it was their penmanship or not to talk so much, the rest of the children now had specific things to look for. I don't have to do it that often, but sometimes I find the need to do something like that.

*Kay:* I find in the older grades that they don't get as stale as often as in the lower grades. They begin to look for academic achievements and socialization skills. I found

141

it helps to pair students. When they sit in pairs, one partner can see what the other partner does.

*Jane:* Let me see if I understand. They have partners, and they look for things they can compliment their partner on? Do you ever have them change partners?

*Kay:* Oh, yes! They send their request in writing to me, and every Tuesday is Changing Partners Day.

*Jane:* What a great idea! This also answers one of the questions about what to do if they're always complimenting the same kid all the time. That's really nice. I hadn't heard of that one before. One that I had heard of is teachers who have kids draw a name out of a hat for a whole week. But I even like this one better. Do they sit by that person for a while?

*Kay:* They sit by that person for a week.

*Jane:* Another possibility is to let them get monotonous at first because they're learning the skill. Once they feel comfortable saying, "I want to compliment him for being my friend," you can start teaching them other things. It helps to focus on looking for what a person *does*—their actions. For example, what do they do to demonstrate their friendship? What specific action would you like to thank them for?

**Question:** What about the message that children often get: I'm a child. This behavior has gotten me what I want out of situations and I wonder if it will work here?

*Jane:* Children do what works, or what they think works. One thing I forgot to mention is that there's nothing wrong with attention. We all want it, and we can get it either usefully or uselessly. There's nothing wrong with power, either. Power can be used negatively or it can be used positively. That's one of the reasons why we want to use class meetings to teach students to use their skills and their decisions in positive, helpful ways. It is our responsibility to teach kids to work on the useful side of life rather than the useless side, because they will do the useless if they perceive that it's working.

**Question:** First-grade students seem only to make suggestions that they've heard before. How can we get first-graders to develop solutions that are more appropriate? Are they developmentally ready to create solutions?

*Janice:* With my first-graders I usually take four suggestions for solutions, and we just talk about those.

*Jane:* Because your kids are coming up with so many, you have to limit it?

*Janice:* Yes, more or less, and that's what they can work with. We talk about whether the solutions are appropriate and how they would work to help people. I think you will find a few students who are going to come up with the same suggestions, but you'll have more suggestions once you get started. You will probably see more problem-solving skills developed.

*Jane:* Part of patience is allowing time. At first the teacher may have to come up with a few suggestions, but the more you learn to keep still and go all the way around the circle, the quicker they're going to start learning what great wisdom and what great ideas they do have. I have found that four-year-olds at family meetings come up with great solutions and great ideas. It's just that we haven't allowed them enough training and experience to know that they can come up with ideas. We're so used to telling kids instead of asking them.

**Question:** How can we make class meetings more than a

tattletale session? It seems that many children thrive on the attention given to them during the session.

*Janice:* I found that with first-graders, I had to give them some guidelines on how to use the agenda. When they put something on the agenda, they have to say why it is a problem to them. Just the other day I had a student put two other names on the agenda because the children were going into each other's desks and taking things. I said, "How does this affect you?" She said, "It doesn't." These two children had agreed that they could each use their pencils or erasers and it really didn't affect her. They had worked out something that was fine. She just thought, "Well, I'm going to tell on them." She had to learn to use the agenda appropriately. One child did a cartwheel in the hall. A student was able to say, "I put it on the agenda because it was not safe. He might get hurt or someone might get kicked." But they have to be able to say why they put it on the agenda.

*Jane:* I think that's a great suggestion—asking them how that affects them. That is very helpful. [This excellent idea has since been incorporated into this book. See Chapters 7 and 8.] Another possibility is to change our feelings about what is a tattletale. What may seem like just tattling to us can be a real problem to them. If we see their concerns as an opportunity to work on solutions instead of tattling, it puts a whole different feeling on their concerns. Usually tattling is, "I want you to punish them," instead of, "This affects me, so how can we solve the problem?" Sometimes teachers like to censor items too much. Janice has found a great way to have the kids censor their own items by asking them how that affects them.

**Question:** What should I do when the same problems come up over and over?

Sometimes teachers decide, "Well, we've already talked about a problem like that, so let's not do it again." That is missing the whole point of the process of class meetings. The fact that Billy hit Janey is not the same to Susie when Dick hits her. You just keep letting them work on solutions. They'll either get better at coming up with the same solution or come up with different ideas. But the main thing is that they feel listened to, they feel taken seriously, and they use their skills. So as long as it affects them, keep letting them work on solutions.

*Kay:* I've also found that they come up with different solutions for different children, because what works for one doesn't work for all. My students are really beginning to look at the individual rather than always just what the problem is, or to say, "We're already discussed it." They begin to look at what will be effective for this person.

*Jane:* I'm so glad you said that. That is such an important point! People are unique. They're individuals. What works for one may not work at all. I love that! And so we can start teaching this to kids. One of the things kids learn in class meetings is that people think differently. They feel differently. They have different ideas. They're not all the same. And, so we start learning to respect differences. [See Chapter 4.]

**Question:** What provisions are made for children with severe discipline problems, children with special needs?

*Kay:* In the two years that I've tried class meetings, if I have any discipline problems, I handle them right there. Fortunately, since I've started class meetings, I've not had any severe problems.

*Jane:* Did you think you had severe problems before you had class meetings?

*Kay:* Yes, and I'm sure I would be having them now if I wasn't doing class meetings. That's one reason I'm so thrilled with class meetings. With the help of the students, we work most things out in our classroom.

*Janet:* I find the same to be true for me. And I think there are still certain things that you as a teacher would have to react to, or if you have a severe discipline problem, maybe refer that child to the proper channels. You would still have to do that even though you're implementing class meetings and trying to solve most of your problems.

*Jane:* I would like to make just a couple of comments about this. I want to tell you two stories. One is a story about a second-grade boy I'll call Stephen. Since Stephen was a foster child, the teacher asked for help from the Foster Youth Office where I worked. She described Stephen as "a severe discipline problem." His classmates were complaining about all the things he did. I strongly believe that class meetings work, no matter what the severity of the behavior. I knew the best way to help this child was through class meetings, but this teacher didn't know how to do class meetings. I thought, okay, we'll accomplish two things at once. We'll help this child, and we'll teach the class-meeting process to the teacher.

I went into the classroom to demonstrate the class meeting. One rule for class meetings is that usually you do not talk about a child unless that child is there. Once you learn that class meetings can be done in a positive, helpful, encouraging, empowering way, then it's safe for kids to talk about anything together. However, in this case I knew these kids hadn't learned to help each other yet. I knew they'd still have that mentality of ganging up and punishing, so we asked Stephen to leave the room.

The first thing I asked the kids was, "What kind of problems are you having with Stephen?" They listed many complaints. I asked, "Do you have any idea why Stephen might do these things?" They said, "Because he's a bully. Because he's mean." Finally one little kid said, "Maybe it's because he's a foster child." I said, "Do you have any idea what it might feel like to be a foster child?" They said, "Gee, you don't have your family. You don't have your same neighborhood." They started feeling compassion.

Then I said, "How many of you would be willing to help Stephen?" Every hand went up. I said, "Okay, what kinds of things could you do to help Stephen? They came up with a long list of things on the board: play with him at recess, walk to and from school with him, have lunch with him, and help him with his work. Then I said, "Okay, who would be willing to do each one of these?" I got specific names after each one of their suggestions.

Later I talked to Stephen. "Stephen, we talked about some of the problems you've been having in class. How many kids do you think wanted to help you?" He said, "Probably none of 'em." I said, "Every one." And he said incredulously, "Every one?" He couldn't believe it.

I want to ask you a question. Do you think Stephen's behavior changed when every kid in that class had changed their way of thinking about him and decided to help? I can guarantee you, his behavior changed significantly. When you help kids understand and get into the helping mode rather than hurting, it makes a huge difference. They are able to accomplish more than any one teacher can do, more than any one foster parent, more than one principal or one counselor. The kids are powerful in what they can do to help.

The next story is regarding a class meeting I visited in San Bernardino, California, and a little boy I'll call Phillip. The class discussed four items while I was there. Three of them had to do with Phillip. I asked Phillip, "Do you feel like the kids are helping you?" He just grinned and said, "Yeah, they're helping me." Later the teacher said

147

to me, "Phillip is still the biggest behavior problem in our class, but the kids do try to help him instead of using him as a scapegoat."

Have you noticed that there is always at least one behavior-problem student in every classroom? Is there anybody who does not have one in your classroom? And have you ever noticed that if that child should happen to move, somebody will gladly take his or her place? There is usually one child who decides to be "special" that way. This teacher said, "The thing I like is that even though Phillip still presents most of the problems, the kids really are working with him in ways that are helpful. They really do try to help him instead of always ganging up and hurting him and putting him down."

**Question:** How do we guide the children into coming up with appropriate logical consequences?

*Janice:* I think just by talking it through with them. One of my favorite examples was with a little boy who put things in his mouth all the time. Somebody put that on the agenda because it wasn't safe: This little boy might choke. One student said, "Well, you should put his color on purple." At that time I had a color chart, and when they got down to purple, they would go see the principal. But another said, "Well, that's not going to do him any good because even if he goes to the principal he's still going to put things in his mouth. He's still going to choke." They were thinking things through.

*Jane:* Because you ask questions like, "How is that going to help?"

*Kay:* I find virtually the same thing with the older child, with the fourth-graders. A lot of times I ask them, "Is this reasonable? And is it related to the problem?" And they really will go back to it and say, "Oh, well, one of these is not related." And they will discuss which ones are not related and mark them off the list. So, they really do a lot of thinking about it before they vote on the consequence.

*Janice:* We have a child that, like you said, is always causing the most trouble. One of the solutions somebody said was, "Well, write to her aunt and tell her." And I knew that they were thinking, "We'll get her in trouble. We'll tell her aunt about this." And I said, "Well, that's a really good idea because maybe we need to have more help. And if we write a letter, we're going to say, 'How can you help us with this problem?' We're *not* going to write the letter to get her in trouble. We just think that maybe if we need more help, then that's another person that we can go to for help." So, we try to put it in a more positive light.

*Kay:* I've also often found that the first time a problem appears on the agenda, their solution to the problem is to stop it. Frequently that's all that's needed. All they need to know is that it is a problem to one of their peers. It is very important to them to have peer approval. If they know that something is displeasing to their peers, many times all they will do is say, "I'll stop it." And it does stop.

*Jane:* So, in other words, sometimes just a discussion is enough. I really want to emphasize this. So often, people focus too much on consequences or solutions without realizing the power of letting the kids discuss it. [See Chapter 9.] After you discuss it you can say, "Okay, if this happens again, it can go on the agenda." But you might be surprised how often it won't happen again.

Asking questions such as, "How will that help?" can be very powerful in teaching kids to consider long-range results. Also, it helps to have the slogan, "We're here to help each other, not to hurt each other." Sometimes you can ask these questions: "How many of you feel like we're coming up with suggestions that are helpful?" "How many of you think we're coming up with suggestions that are hurtful?" A key technique, whenever you see things going wrong, is to ask a question. But ask it both ways: "How many of you think we're being too noisy?" "How many of you think it's quiet enough?" "How many of you think we're being respectful?" "How many of you think we're being disrespectful?" Asking questions invites them to think.

**Question:** How do we handle children who use the agenda as revenge?

*Kay:* In the beginning, I did my agenda as Jane had suggested in *Positive Discipline* by using a big chart paper. [Some classes use an agenda book, some a piece of paper posted on the bulletin board, and some simply write on the corner of the blackboard.] I did find that the children used the agenda for revenge all the time. So I came up with an agenda box. It has a hole in the top, and they just simply put their agenda item in the box. They created a number system. They put a number on the problem (and then crossed off the number they used so the next person will know which number to use), and we take them in order at the class meeting. So it works beautifully! The children love this, and they're in charge of taking care of it all. I don't do any of it.

*Jane:* I just love how much I keep learning from teachers! With this system you can keep problems that go in the box in order. That's brilliant!

*Janice:* I don't notice that first-graders use the agenda for revenge. I just find that first-graders are pretty honest

Usually, a classmate will check on them and say, "She just did that to get back." When I confront them, they'll usually say, "Yeah, I did." I always like to thank them or give them credit for admitting something like that right away.

*Jane:* Any one of these questions could go on the agenda. You could ask them, "What should we do about people using the agenda for revenge?" They will come up with great answers. But the other thing is that whenever you have a problem, talk about it openly with the kids.

Another way to handle the kids using the agenda for revenge is to say, "I've noticed that we're using the agenda for revenge." Then I would ask some questions like, "How many think that we don't trust each other yet to know that we're here to help each other rather than hurt each other?" Getting the students involved in solutions or a simple discussion is usually enough to stop the revenge.

**Question:** What do you suggest for a student whose name is on the agenda frequently?

*Janice:* That happened last year, and the children solved it really beautifully at a class meeting. This year, it happened again. One little girl's name was on every day. I could see she was trying. She was making an effort. And I said, "What do you think if this child sees her name on the agenda every day, even though she's trying? How would you feel about that? Even though you knew that you were trying real hard every day, somebody's still going to complain about you?" They said they wouldn't like it. That was one of the only times I've said not to put something on the agenda. Instead the class decided to give her two weeks to really try, without putting her name on the agenda.

*Jane:* What a beautiful way to handle that witht he kids. How would you feel if this was happening to you?

That is such a good way to help them really start thinking and develop a consciousness about how their behavior
affects other people.

*Kay:* With the older children we just talk about it. We
say, "How would you feel if your name kept coming up
all the time? And is this student really working on it?" And
then, if they're in their mood of doing negative consequences, which sometimes the older children will get into,
we start saying, "Let's really concentrate on helpful suggestions." They will switch gears and really do some helpful
things.

**Question:** How do you incorporate other discipline
strategies with the Positive Discipline program?

*Jane:* I have a generic answer for that: It fits any other
discipline program that treats kids with dignity and
respect, that is not humiliating, that works for solutions
rather than blame, and that teaches skills rather than
punishment and control. It does not fit discipline pro-
grams that are based on a punishment/reward premise.
That is a totally opposite premise. Those systems teach
adults to be responsible for kids' behavior by catching kids
when they're "good" and rewarding them and catching
kids when they're "bad" and punishing them. But what
happens when the adult is not around? It also is a short-
term control, rather than taking a look at what children
are feeling and deciding and what kind of skills they are
learning for future behavior.

*Jane:* Do you want to make any closing comments?
I would like to hear from both of you, just a summariza-
tion about what you think about the whole thing.

*Kay:* Holding regularly scheduled class meetings is
one of the most wonderful things that's ever happened

to me in my classroom, and my students feel the same way. They love it! They fuss if we miss a class meeting. I have class meetings every day. Once in a while our schedule becomes so hectic we just can't work it in that day, and they really miss it. I find that my classroom operates much more smoothly if we have the opportunity to have the compliments. If we don't have time for anything except compliments, even that makes the day run much more smoothly.

*Jane:* I'm so glad you mentioned that. So many teachers say that the whole day runs more smoothly when they do have class meetings even if it's only the compliment part.

*Janice:* I love class meetings. I urge everyone to try it. I never felt comfortable with the discipline program we had when I came into the system. I was so glad to be able to take something that would replace it. I have nothing in place in my classroom now for discipline *except* class meetings.

We hope this transcript has captured the expertise, positive attitude, and outstanding skills of Janice Ritter and Kay Rogers. We believe their example will be an inspiration to thousands of teachers who see the potential of class meetings for empowering students and creating a cooperative classroom climate. We hope you, too, will be motivated by their experience to start class meetings and enjoy the fruits of this powerful process for teachers and students alike.

# APPENDIX
# A

# Teachers-Helping-Teachers Problem-Solving Steps

Teachers wishing to establish positive discipline in their classrooms have found that they need encouragement regularly. When teachers hold weekly, monthly, or bi-monthly meetings with each other, they work better with their students and are more successful in the classroom.

We recommend that each meeting be divided into two parts. In the first part, hold an open discussion deal-ing with any aspect of the Positive Discipline program. In the second part, usually the last half hour, follow the problem-solving steps presented here to get help with specific problems in class or with a student. Each time the teachers get together, one of the teachers can volunteer to share a real problem he or she is having in the class-room. Another teacher can be a facilitator using the fol-lowing step-by-step approach to come up with a solution that can be tried for one week.

There are two versions of the Teachers-Helping-Teachers Problem-Solving Steps: (1) a short version that can be transferred to a poster and serve as a guide at a teachers' meeting, and (2) an expanded version, which provides a broader base for the teacher facilitating the problem-solving process at a teacher's meeting.

Following is the expanded version of the Teachers-Helping-Teachers Problem-Solving Steps. These directions are for the person who is the facilitator of the process. The short version, which can be posted so everyone can follow along can be found in Appendix B. We also recommend posting the Mistaken Goal Chart in Appendix C.

The Teachers-Helping-Teachers Problem-Solving Steps serve as an intake, an assessment, a diagnostic tool, a treatment plan, an action plan, and an encouragement process all rolled into one. These steps are effective because they give teachers practical ideas and skills that work for positive change. Going through the steps with other teachers is fun and nonthreatening. It eliminates the endless analysis that often focuses on causes, blame, and excuses instead of helpful action.

▼ 1. Invite the volunteer teacher to sit next to you and explain to him or her the Teachers-Helping-Teachers Problem-Solving Steps.

The volunteer teacher sits next to you because he or she is a co-helper with you in this process. This way, you can offer encouragement with your friendly energy. Also, you can put your hand on a knee or shoulder in a friendly manner when you need to interrupt. Closeness will help you read subtle body language, facial expressions, and tone of voice.

Explain to the volunteer teacher, "The Teachers-Helping-Teachers Problem-Solving Steps is a process we can use to solve a school situation that isn't working well. Not only will you get help, but you will help others who watch the process because they will see something of themselves in the situation you describe. They will also be able to use some of the suggestions we create for your situation for their own situations. Thank you for volunteering to be a volunteer co-teacher with me in this process."

▼ 2. Introduce the volunteer teacher. On a flip-chart, write the volunteer teacher's name, teaching grade level, and number of kids in class. (Birth order of teacher is optional.) Write the student's name, age, and birth order.

When looking at the birth order of the teacher and the student, it can be fun to alert the group to some possibilities they could look for based on birth order. For example if the teacher is the oldest sibling in the family, are perfectionism and bossiness a problem? (Joke with the teacher: "We know you wouldn't have these characteristics, but some other first-born teachers might.") You might ask, "Are you sometimes too hard on yourself when things don't go as well as you would like?" This often helps a first-born person feel understood. For those who are middle-born, is trying to save the world a problem? They often see all sides to every issue and get caught up in what's fair. They often work well with rebels and underdogs. For teachers born last in their family, is a lack of order a problem, or are they waiting for someone else to fix things for them? They often allow for lots of creativity. A teacher who is an only child may be similar to an oldest or youngest.

You can also make some guesses about the student based on birth order. Is a youngest student looking for special service, a middle student looking for a place by being different, an oldest giving up because he or she can't be first, or an only child having trouble sharing? There may not be time to spend on this issue, but leaders should be aware of it. [See Chapter 3 for more information on birth order.]

▼ 3. Ask for a brief statement of the problem. (If the teacher goes on and on, interrupt and say, "It's time to move on.") Ask the group to raise hands to see if anyone else has ever had a similar problem.

In this step, you are looking for a general idea of the problem, not the details. Sometimes a teacher may give too much detail. Interrupt and say, "If you could describe the problem in one word or one sentence, what would it be?"

It's important to ask the group if they have a similar problem. It is very encouraging for the teacher to not feel alone or inadequate by knowing others are in the same boat.

▼ 4. Ask the teacher to describe the last time the problem occurred in enough detail and dialogue so that the group can get an idea of how to role-play the situation.

In this step, you are looking for a specific example of the problem. Unless you focus on one incident, you, the teacher, and everyone involved will get overwhelmed and go away without satisfactory help. One episode represents a microcosm of what occurs between this teacher and student. Focusing on and understanding the single incident will help them with all other similar situations.

Asking for a description that includes details and dialogue for role players helps the teacher focus on the incident instead of telling stories about background and causes.

▼ 5. If feelings weren't expressed in the above description, ask the teacher, "How did you feel?" Ask the group, "How many of you have ever felt that way?"

It is important for the teacher to express feelings, because they give us clues about the belief behind the student's behavior, which we call the student's mistaken goal. If appropriate, you can explain to the group, "What the teacher feels gives us the clue to the student's mistaken goal. For example, if the teacher feels annoyed, this is a clue that the student's mistaken goal is undue attention." Some people get this confused and think you have to know what the *student* feels in order to understand his or her goal.

Most people are not used to identifying their own feelings. Explain that it takes only one word to describe a feeling. If the teacher is going on and on about what he or she thinks instead of what he or she feels, or if he or she comes up with a vague feeling like "frustrated," use the Mistaken Goal Chart and ask the teacher to find a feeling in the first column that comes closest to describing their own.

Again, it is important to check with the group to see if they have felt the same, so that the teacher is encouraged by knowing others feel the same.

▼  6. Ask, "What did you do?" "What did the student do?" "Then what happened?" "What happened next?" "How did you feel in response to what the student did?"

These answers may have come out in the initial description of the incident. If not, they are important because they help you find more clues about the mistaken goal. What the teacher did, and the student's response to what the teacher did, provide more clues about the mistaken goal and thus the reason for the student's misbehaving. For example, if the student stops the behavior for a while in response to what the teacher did but starts up again a few hours or days later, the mistaken goal is probably undue attention. If the student resists cooperation (actively or passively), the goal is probably power.

▼  7. Ask, "Did it work?" "Want to try something new?"

If it had worked, there wouldn't be a problem, and the teacher wouldn't be asking for help. But, these questions are important to verify, clarify, and substantiate a commitment to trying something else. Help the teacher conclude from known results that more of the same won't produce different results by joking, "Have you heard the definition of insanity? Doing the same thing over and over and expecting a different result. Only adults do that. Kids

159

are smart enough to keep doing what works for them or try something else if what they do doesn't work."

▼ 8. Using the Mistaken Goals Chart, [see Appendix C] see if you can guess why the student's mistaken goal may be based on the teacher's feelings, and what the student did in response to what the teacher did. If it isn't obvious from expressed feelings, ask the teacher to look at the Mistaken Goal Chart, and choose the feeling that comes closest to the words in the first column.

This may have come out as part of Step 5. Don't spend a lot of time trying to figure out the goal, especially if the conversation turns to analysis. Say, "Let's see what more information we get from the role-play." Even if you never know for sure what the mistaken goal is, people will get help from the role playing and brainstorming.

▼ 9. Set up the role-play.

Use your intuition to determine which role the teacher should play in order to learn the most. As a general rule, it's helpful for the teacher to role-play the student, to *get into the student's world*. Sometimes it might be best for the teacher to watch the role-play instead. Later, when role-playing the suggested solution, it's usually best to have the teacher play himself or herself to practice the skill of the new suggestion. Again, you might feel it best for the teacher to watch or experience the student's reaction to the suggestion. Assign someone to play each part. Have four to six people represent students in the classroom. Tell them to start with the dialogue they heard during the description of the problem.

Some facilitators are afraid some people might object to role playing, and some people do. But a facilitator who is confident about the value of role playing won't be discouraged by the resistance. Proceed to set up the role-play with confidence. When you ask for volunteers to play roles, be quiet and wait. Someone will fill the void of silence and volunteer. You might joke with them in your own way, or say, "I feel resistance. It reminds me of my resistance before I found out how valuable this is and how much fun it can be. Okay, who are the brave souls who are going to jump in and help me show how much fun this is?"

Set up the room to represent the real situation. Are the desks in rows or groupings? Is the teacher in the front of the room or somewhere else? It's important to have a few people represent the rest of the kids in the class because they'll show how one person's behavior affects everyone else.

To get the role-play started, remind someone of their opening line, or ask the volunteer teacher to remind someone of an opening line.

▼ 10. Process the role-play.

Stop the players as soon as you think they've had enough time to experience feelings and decisions (usually less than a minute). Ask the players, one at a time, what they were feeling and what they were deciding as the people they were playing. This information sheds more light on the problem, and the processing serves as a debriefing for role players who may be left with a lot of stirred-up feelings they need to express. Asking the students what they are deciding helps teachers see the long-range results of their actions instead of just the immediate result. Remember, feelings can usually be expressed in one word, and they happen inside us.

▼ 11. Brainstorm with the group for possible solutions the teacher could try.

Write down all suggestions on the flip-chart. Ask everyone in the group to refer to the alternative column on the Mistaken Goal Chart [see Appendix C] for suggestions, or make suggestions from their personal experience.

Brainstorming allows each person to participate. It helps people accept and value how easy it can be to solve other people's problems. When it's someone else's problem, we are not emotionally involved, so we have objectivity and perspective. Once we accept this, we can appreciate the value of being consultants to each other instead of thinking we should be able to solve all our own problems—or that we are failures if we even admit we *have* a problem.

Encourage the group to think of as many alternatives as possible. Make if safe for them to make suggestions by respecting and writing down each suggestion on the flip-chart. This is not a time for discussion or asking questions of the volunteer teacher, nor is it time to analyze any of the suggestions with the volunteer teacher.

Suggestions will improve as teachers learn to use more of the tools described in this book. Do not censor negative suggestions. If a negative suggestion is chosen, be sure there is time to role-play it, so they can learn the results from what the person playing the student feels and decides in response to the teacher's.

▼   12. Ask the teacher to choose a suggestion to try for one week. Ask a volunteer to write down the chosen suggestion on a sheet of paper and hand it to the teacher.

▼   13. Role-play the chosen suggestion.

This time, have the teacher play herself or himself. Some teachers prefer just to watch, while some prefer to play the student, to get that perspective. This is a good chance for the teacher to practice the chosen suggestion. Many times we'll have a good idea, but when we try to apply it, we incorporate some of our old habits (such as lecturing, controlling, a little humiliation thrown in) and then wonder why it didn't work. All this will come out in the role-play, and those watching will also gain some insight about why some of the things they do may not be working.

If the chosen suggestion is a negative one, the role-play will demonstrate why it doesn't work when you process the student's feelings and decisions. It is important to ask all role players what they were feeling and deciding in order to learn how a situation affects everyone. Finding out that a chosen suggestion won't work does not mean the time has been wasted. Everyone will learn many valuable things during the process.

▼ 14. Ask for the teacher's commitment to try the suggestion for one week and to report back to the group at the following meeting.

Let the teacher know how important it is for the group to hear the results of their efforts so they can know how suggestions work in the real world. (We recommend regularly scheduled meetings for teachers, no less than once a month and preferably once a week while they are learning these new skills.)

▼ 15. Ask the group for appreciations for the volunteer teacher.

What help did you get for yourself by watching this? What did you see that you appreciate about the volunteer? What ideas did you see that you could use? This is the time to give back to the volunteer by telling him or her what she gave to you. Appreciations may sound like this: "I learned . . . " "I felt . . . " "I have the same problem, so now I can try . . . " "I know how hard it is to share . . ." "Thank you for . . . "

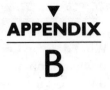

▼
**APPENDIX**

# B

# Problem-Solving Steps (Short Version)

1. Invite the volunteer teacher to sit next to you and explain the Teachers-Helping-Teachers Problem-Solving Steps.

2. Introduce the volunteer teacher. On a flip-chart, write the volunteer teacher's name, teaching grade level, and number of kids in class. (Birth order of teacher is optional.) Write the student's name, age, and birth order.

3. Ask for a brief statement of the problem. Ask the group to raise hands to see if anyone else has ever had a similar problem.

4. Ask the teacher to describe the last time the problem occurred in enough detail and dialogue so that the group can get an idea of how to role-play the situation.

5. Ask the teacher, "How did you feel?" Ask the group, "How many of you have ever felt that way?"

6. Ask, "What did you do?" "What did the student do?" "Then what happened?" "What happened next?" "How did you feel in response to what the student did?"

7. Ask, "Did it work?" "Want to try something new?"

8. Guess the student's mistaken goal using the Mistaken Goal Chart.

9. Set up and perform role-play.

10. Process the role-play by asking players to share feelings and decisions.

11. Brainstorm for possible solutions.

12. Ask the teacher to choose a suggestion.

13. Role-play the chosen suggestion.

14. Ask for the teacher's commitment to try the suggestion for one week.

15. Ask the group for appreciations for the volunteer teacher.

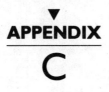

# Mistaken Goal Chart

| If the Parent/ Teacher Feels | And Tends to React by | And if the Child's Response Is to | The Child's Goal Is | The Belief Behind the Child's Behavior Is | Parent/Teacher Alternatives Include |
|---|---|---|---|---|---|
| Annoyed Irritated Worried Guilty | Reminding Coaxing Doing things for the child he/she could do for him/herself. | Stop temporarily, but later resume same or another disturbing behavior | Undue attention (to keep others busy with him) | I count (belong) only when I'm being noticed or getting special service. I'm only important when I'm keeping you busy with me. | "I like you and _____." (Example: I care about you and will spend time with you later.) Give positive attention at other times. Avoid special service. Say it only once, then act. Plan special time. Set up routines. Take time for training. Use natural and logical consequences. Encourage. Redirect. Use family/class meetings. Touch without words. Ignore. Set up nonverbal signals. |
| Angry Provoked Challenged Threatened Defeated | Fighting Giving in Thinking, "You can't get away with it." "I'll make you." Wanting to be right | Intensify behavior Act with defiant compliance Feels he/she's won when parents/teachers are upset Passive power | Power (to be boss) | I belong only when I'm boss or in control or proving no one can boss me. "You can't make me." | Ask for help. Don't fight and don't give in. Withdraw from conflict. Do the unexpected. Be firm and kind. Act, don't talk. Decide what you will do. Let routines be the boss. Leave and calm down. Develop mutual respect. Give limited choices. Set reasonable and few limits. Practice follow-through. Encourage. Redirect to positive power. Use family/class meetings. |
| Hurt Disappointed Disbelieving Disgusted | Retaliating Getting even Thinking, "How could you do this to me?" | Retaliate Intensify Escalates the same behavior or chooses another weapon | Revenge (to get even) | I don't think I belong so I'll hurt others as I feel hurt. I can't be liked or loved. | Deal with the hurt feelings. Avoid punishment and retaliation. Build trust. Use reflective listening. Share your feelings. Make amends. Show you care. Act, don't talk. Encouragement of strengths. Put kids in same boat. Use family/class meetings. |
| Despair Hopeless Helpless | Giving up Doing for Overhelping | Retreat further Passive No improvement No response | Assumed disability (to give up and be left alone) | I can't belong because I'm not perfect, so I'll convince others not to expect anything of me. I am helpless and unable; it's no use trying because I won't do it right. | Show faith. Take small steps. Stop all criticism. Encourage any positive attempt, no matter how small. Focus on assets. Don't pity. Don't give up. Set up opportunities for success. Teach skills/show how. Step back. Enjoy the child. Build on their interests. Encourage, encourage, encourage. Use family/class meetings. |

▼

# Bibliography

Adler, Alfred. *Cooperation Between the Sexes.* New York: Anchor Books, 1978.

——. *Social Interest.* New York: Capricorn Books, 1964.

——. *Superiority and Social Interest.* Evanston, IL: Northwestern University Press, 1964.

——. *What Life Should Mean to You.* New York: Capricorn Books, 1958.

Albert, Linda. *Coping with Kids.* New York: E. P. Dutton, 1982.

Allred, G. Hugh. *How to Strengthen Your Marriage and Family.* Provo, UT: Brigham Young University Press, 1976.

——. *Mission for Mother: Guiding the Child.* Salt Lake City, UT: Book Crafts, 1968.

Ansbacher, Heinz and Rowena. *The Individual Psychology of Alfred Adler.* New York: Harper Torchbooks, 1964.

Bayard, Robert and Jean. *How to Deal with Your Acting Up Teenager.* San Jose, CA: The Accord Press, 1981.

Beecher, Willard and Marguerite. *Beyond Success and Failure.* New York: Pocket Books, 1966.

Bettner, Betty Lou, and Amy Lew. *Raising Kids Who Can.* New York: HarperCollins, 1992.

Christianson, Oscar. *Adlerian Family Counseling.* Minneapolis, MN: Educational Media Corp., 1983.

Corsini, Raymond, and Genevieve Painter. *The Practical Parent.* New York: Harper and Row, 1975.

Corsini, Raymond, and Clinton Phillips. *Give In or Give Up.* Chicago: Nelson Hall, 1982.

Deline, John. *Who's Raising the Family?* Madison, WI: Wisconsin Clearing House, 1981.

Dinkmeyer, Don, and Rudolf Dreikurs. *Encouraging Children to Learn: The Encouragement Process.* Englewood Cliffs, NJ: Prentice-Hall, 1963.

Dinkmeyer, Don, and Gary McKay. *Parents Handbook: Systematic Training for Effective Parenting,* 3rd edition. Circle Pines, MN: American Guidance Service, Inc., 1989.

——. *Raising a Responsible Child.* New York: Simon & Schuster, 1973.

Dinkmeyer, Don, W. L. Pew, and Don Dinkmeyer. *Adlerian Counseling and Psychotherapy.* Monterey, CA: Brooks/Cole Publishing, 1979.

Dreikurs, Rudolf. *Psychology in the Classroom.* New York: Harper and Row, 1966.

——. *Social Equality: The Challenge of Today.* Chicago: Contemporary Books, Inc., 1971.

Dreikurs, Rudolf, Raymond Corsini, and S. Gould. *Family Council.* Chicago: Henry Regnery, 1974.

Dreikurs, Rudolf, Bernice Grunwald, and Floyd Pepper. *Maintaining Sanity in the Classroom.* New York: Harper and Row, 1971.

Dreikurs, Rudolf, and V. Soltz. *Children: The Challenge.* New York: Dutton, 1964.

Dyer, Wayne. *Your Erroneous Zones.* New York: Avon Books, 1976.

Glenn, H. Stephen. *Bridging Troubled Waters* (Audio Cassette Tape Set). Fair Oaks, CA: Sunrise Press, 1989. (1/800/456-7770)

——. *Developing Capable People* (Audio Cassette Tape Set). Fair Oaks, CA: Sunrise Press. (1/800/456-7770)

——. *Developing Healthy Self-Esteem* (Video Tape). Fair Oaks, CA: Sunrise Productions, 1989. (1/800/456-7770)

——. *Empowering Others: Ten Keys to Affirming and Validating People* (Video Tape). Fair Oaks, CA: Sunrise Productions, 1989. (1/800/456-7770)

——. *The Greatest Human Need* (Video Tape). Fair Oaks, CA: Sunrise Productions, 1989. (1/800/456-7770)

——. *Introduction to Developing Capable People* (Video Tape). Fair Oaks, CA: Sunrise Productions, 1989. (1/800/456-7770)

——. *Involving and Motivating People* (Audio Cassette Tape). Fair Oaks, CA: Sunrise Press. (1/800/456-7770)

——. *Six Steps to Developing Responsibility* (Video Tape). Fair Oaks, CA: Sunrise Productions, 1989. (1/800/456-7770)

————. *Teachers Who Make a Difference* (Video Tape). Fair Oaks, CA: Sunrise Productions, 1989. (1/800/456-7770)

————. *What They See Is What You've Got: Five Keys to Working with Perception* (Video Tape). Fair Oaks, CA: Sunrise Productions, 1989. (1/800/456-7770)

Glenn, H. Stephen, and Jane Nelsen. *Raising Self-Reliant Children in a Self-Indulgent World.* Rocklin, CA: Prima Publishing, 1988. (1/916/756-0426)

Goldberg, Herb. *Hazards of Being Male.* New American Library, 1976.

Janoe, Ed and Barbara. *About Anger.* Vancouver, WA: Arco Press, 1973.

————. *Dealing with Feelings.* Vancouver, WA: Arco Press, 1973.

Kvols-Riedler, Bill and Kathy. *Redirecting Children's Misbehavior.* Boulder, CO: R.D.I.C. Publications, 1979.

Losoney, Lewis. *You Can Do It.* Englewood Cliffs, NJ: Prentice-Hall, 1980.

Lott, Lynn. *Changing Your Relationship with Your Teen.* Santa Rosa, CA: The Practical Press, 1987. (707/526-3141)

————. *Family Work: Whose Job Is It?* Santa Rosa, CA: The Practical Press, 1983. (707/526-3141).

————. *Married and Liking It.* Santa Rosa, CA: The Practical Press, 1987. (707/526-3141)

————. *To Know Me Is to Love Me.* Santa Rosa, CA: The Practical Press, 1983. (707/526-3141)

Lott, Lynn, and Jane Nelsen. *Teaching Parenting.* Fair Oaks, CA: Sunrise Press, 1990.

Manaster, Guy J., and Raymond Corsini. *Individual Psychology.* Itasca, IL: F. E. Peacock Publishers, Inc., 1982.

Nelsen, Jane. *Positive Discipline.* New York: Ballantine Books, 1987. Originally published in 1981 by Sunrise Press, Fair Oaks, CA. (1/800/456-7770)

————. *Positive Discipline* (Audio Cassette Tape). Fair Oaks, CA: Sunrise Press. (1/800/456-7770)

————. *Positive Discipline Study Guide.* Fair Oaks, CA: Sunrise Press, 1988. (1/800/456-7770)

————. *Positive Discipline Video.* Fair Oaks, CA: Sunrise Press, 1988. (1/800/456-7770)

————. *Understanding: Eliminating Stress and Finding Serenity in Life and Relationships.* Rocklin, CA: Prima Publishing, 1988. Originally published in 1986 by Sunrise Press, Fair Oaks, CA. (1/800/456-7770)

Nelsen, Jane, and H. Stephen Glenn. *Time Out*. Fair Oaks, CA: Sunrise Press, 1991.

Nelsen, Jane, Riki Intner, and Lynn Lott. *Clean and Sober Parenting*. Rocklin, CA: Prima Publishing, 1992.

Nelsen, Jane, and Lynn Lott. *I'm On Your Side*. Rocklin, CA: Prima Publishing, 1990.

Pew, W. L., and J. Terner. *Courage to Be Imperfect*. New York: Hawthorn Books, 1978.

Smith, Manuel J. *When I Say No I Feel Guilty*. New York: The Dial Press, 1975.

Walton, F. X. *Winning Teenagers Over*. Columbia, SC: Adlerian Child Care Books.

# Index

# BOOKS AND TAPES BY JANE NELSEN, LYNN LOTT AND H. STEPHEN GLENN

To:  Sunrise Books, Tapes & Videos, Box B, Provo, UT 84603    Phone: 1-800-456-7770

| BOOKS | Price | Quantity | Amount |
|---|---|---|---|
| *POSITIVE DISCIPLINE IN THE CLASSROOM* by Nelsen, Lott & Glenn | $14.95 | | |
| *RAISING SELF-RELIANT CHILDREN IN A SELF-INDULGENT WORLD* by Glenn & Nelsen | $9.95 | | |
| *I'M ON YOUR SIDE* by Nelsen & Lott | $9.95 | | |
| *POSITIVE DISCIPLINE* by Nelsen | $9.95 | | |
| *TIME OUT* by Nelsen & Glenn | $6.95 | | |
| *UNDERSTANDING* by Nelsen | $9.95 | | |
| *CLEAN AND SOBER PARENTING* by Nelsen, Riki Intner & Lott | $10.95 | | |
| *TO KNOW ME IS TO LOVE ME* by Lott, Marilyn Kentz & Dru West | $10.00 | | |
| *FAMILY WORK: WHOSE JOB IS IT?* by Lott, Intner & Kientz | $9.95 | | |
| *TOGETHER AND LIKING IT* by Lott and West | $7.95 | | |
| **MANUALS** | | | |
| *POSITIVE DISCIPLINE IN THE CLASSROOM FACILITATOR'S GUIDE* by Nelsen, Lott and Glenn | $39.95 | | |
| *DEVELOPING CAPABLE PEOPLE MANUAL* by Glenn and Nelsen *Leader's Guide* | $59.95 | | |
| *Participant's Workbook* | $6.95 | | |
| *TEACHING PARENTING MANUAL* by Lott and Nelsen | $39.95 | | |
| *EMPOWERING PARENTS OF TEENS* by Nelsen, Lott, Beverly Berna & Ellen Spurlock | $29.95 | | |
| **CASSETTE TAPES** | | | |
| *POSITIVE DISCIPLINE IN THE CLASSROOM* by Nelsen, Lott & Glenn (six-tape set) | $49.95 | | |
| *DEVELOPING CAPABLE PEOPLE* by Glenn (six-tape set) | $49.95 | | |
| *EMPOWERING TEENAGERS AND YOURSELF IN THE PROCESS* by Nelsen and Lott (seven-tape set) | $49.95 | | |
| *POSITIVE DISCIPLINE* by Nelsen | $10.00 | | |

SUBTOTAL _____

UT residents add 6.25% sales tax; CA residents add 7.25% sales tax _____

Shipping & Handling: $2.50 plus 50¢ for each item _____

TOTAL _____

(Prices subject to change without notice.)

METHOD OF PAYMENT (check one):

_____ Check made payable to SUNRISE, INC. _____ Mastercard _____ Visa

Card #_____ _____ _____ _____ Expiration _____/_____

Ship to_____

Address_____

City/State/Zip_____

Daytime Phone_____

**For a free newsletter, call toll-free: 1-800-456-7770**